THE KURDISTAN REGION
OF IRAQ

THE KURDISTAN REGION
OF IRAQ

*Assessing the Economic and Social Impact
of the Syrian Conflict and ISIS*

 **WORLD BANK GROUP**

ISBN (paper): 978-1-4648-0548-6
ISBN (electronic): 978-1-4648-0549-3
DOI: 10.1596/978-1-4648-0548-6

Cover photo: Displaced people, fleeing violence from forces loyal to the Islamic State in Sinjar town, walk toward the Syrian border on the outskirts of Sinjar Mountain. © Reuters/Rodi Said. Used with the permission of Reuters/Rodi Said. Further permission required for reuse.

Cover Design: Bill Pragluski, Critical Stages, LLC.

Library of Congress Cataloging-in-Publication Data has been requested.

Contents

Maps

Photos

Tables

Acknowledgments

This report was written by a team led by Sibel Kulaksiz (task team leader and senior economist) and composed of Janet Dooley (senior country officer), Nazaneen Ali (senior procurement specialist), Sepehr Fotovat (senior procurement specialist), Cevdet Denizer (consultant), Harun Onder (economist), Aaditya Mattoo (research manager), Shahrzad Mobasher Fard (consultant), Tracy Hart (senior environmental specialist), Ibrahim Dajani (senior operations officer), Soran Ali (operations officer), Said Dahdah (transport specialist), Igor Jokanovic (consultant), Ferhat Esen (senior energy specialist), Nafie Mofid (water supply specialist), Amal Talbi (senior water and sanitation specialist), Caroline Bahnson (consultant), Lina Abdallah (urban specialist), Tamer Rabie (senior health specialist), Firas Raad (senior health specialist), Samira Nikaein (consultant), Moukim Temourov (senior economist, education), Ramzi Afif Neman (consultant), Ghassan Alkhoja (senior social protection specialist), Ray Salvatore Jennings (senior social development consultant), Guillemette Jaffrin (senior private sector development specialist), Bertine Kamphuis (private sector development specialist), Teymour Abdel Aziz (economist), Peter McConaghy (consultant), Nandini Krishnan (senior economist), Sergio Olivieri (economist), and Shomikho Raha (social development specialist).

The task team was supported by Robert Bou Jaoude (country manager), Kevin Carey (lead economist), Eric Le Borgne (lead economist), Husam Mohamed Beides (program leader), Haneen Sayed (program leader), Peter Mousley (program leader), Niels Harild (manager, Global Program on Forced Displacement), Charles Cormier (practice manager, energy and extractives), Yolanda Tayler (practice manager, procurement), Luis Prada (senior procurement specialist), Caroline van den Berg (lead water and sanitation specialist), and Steven Schonberger (practice manager, water sector).

The report was prepared under the overall guidance and supervision of Ferid Belhaj (director, Middle East and North Africa Department) and Bernard Funck (practice manager, Macroeconomics and Fiscal Management). The report benefited from comments by peer reviewers Martin Raiser (country director for Turkey), Sudharshan Canagarajah (operations adviser), and Nadia Fernanda Piffaretti (senior economist).

The team is grateful for the close collaboration and the strong engagement of the KRG authorities under the leadership of the Ministry of Planning. Overall guidance and coordination from the government was provided by Mr. Ali Sindi, Minister of Planning, and Mr. Zagros Siwaily, Director General, Ministry of Planning. The World Bank team extends their deepest gratitude to all government officials for excellent collaboration.

Abbreviations

CBI	Central Bank of Iraq
CCCM	Camp Coordination and Camp Management
CPI	consumer price index
DoH	Department of Health
EIU	Economist Intelligence Unit
ESIA	Economic and Social Impact Assessment
EU	European Union
FAO	Food and Agriculture Organization
GDP	gross domestic product
GDRB	General Directorate for Roads and Bridges
GRP	gross regional product
HGV	heavy goods vehicle
HH	household
HMIS	Health Management and Information System
ICU	intensive care unit
IDP	internally displaced person
IHSES	Iraq Household Socioeconomic Survey
IMF	International Monetary Fund
IOM	International Organization for Migration
IPP	independent power producer
IRP	Immediate Response Plan
ISIS	Islamic State in Iraq and Syria
KRG	Kurdistan Regional Government
KRI	Kurdistan Region of Iraq
KRSO	Kurdistan Regional Statistics Office
LGV	light goods vehicle
LOS	level of service
MCH	maternal and child health
MDER	Minimum Dietary Energy Requirement
MENA	Middle East and North Africa

MFI	microfinance institution
MoE	Ministry of Electricity
MoHC	Ministry of Housing and Construction
MOLSA	Ministry of Labor and Social Affairs
MSW	Municipal Solid Waste
NGO	nongovernmental organization
NSWMP	National Solid Waste Management Plan
O&M	operations and maintenance
OECD	Organisation for Economic Co-operation and Development
PAR	portfolio at risk
PDS	Public Distribution System
PHC	primary health care
PPA	power purchase agreement
RAND	Research and Development Corporation
REACH	Responsive Education for All Children
SEINA	Socio-Economic Infrastructure Needs Assessment
SME	small and medium enterprise
SPSF	Social Protection Strategic Framework
TB	tuberculosis
UN	United Nations
UNDP	United Nations Development Programme
UNHCR	United Nations High Commissioner for Refugees
UNICEF	United Nations Children's Fund
WDR	World Development Report
WFP	World Food Program
WHO	World Health Organization

Currency equivalents, exchange rate as of February 7, 2015:
US$1 = ID (Iraqi dinar) 1,166; ID 1 = $0.000858

Fiscal year is January 1 to December 31

Overview

At the request of the prime minister of the Kurdistan Regional Government (KRG), H. E. Nechervan Barzani, this Economic and Social Impact Assessment (ESIA) seeks to identify and, where feasible, quantify the impact of the recent regional crises on KRG and the required stabilization costs for 2015. The following events motivated this study: the Syrian civil war, which began in 2011, and the insurgency of the ISIS (Islamic State in Iraq and Syria) group, which began in June 2014. The violence and atrocities associated with both of these events caused tens of thousands of people to flee their homes, and many chose the relative safety of the Kurdistan Region of Iraq (KRI), as refugees from the Syrian conflict and as internally displaced persons (IDPs) from the ISIS crisis. These events took place in the context of the fiscal crisis, which caused a drop of about 90 percent in fiscal transfers from the central government in Baghdad starting in early 2014. This report provides KRG with a technical assessment of the impact and stabilization costs associated with the influx of refugees and IDPs. *Impact* refers to the immediate economic and fiscal effects on the KRG economy and budget, whereas *stabilization cost* refers to the additional spending needed to restore the welfare of residents of KRI. The report is the outcome of a process in which a World Bank team engaged intensively on the ground with regional government institutions and international partners to gather and mobilize data from disparate sources into a structured narrative and integrated technical presentation from which all stakeholders can draw to help them design and implement strategies for coping with the crisis.

This rapid ESIA at the subregional level differs from standard needs assessments because of the nature of the shocks with which KRG is dealing for the following reasons. First, the crisis in KRI is still unfolding and continues to be affected by events in Syria and the rest of Iraq, but it is neither a postconflict nor a postdisaster condition. Second, the duration and magnitude of the crisis are uncertain, and hence the real impact of the shock depends on and will continue to depend on conditions in Syria and Iraq. Third, no significant material damage has occurred to KRI's infrastructure, its human and physical capital stocks, or its housing. As such, the impact of shocks has affected flow measures of economic activity such as gross domestic product (GDP) growth rate, incomes, and local and foreign direct investment, as well as the provision and access to public goods and services to the population. This subregional ESIA is a rapid assessment that provides a snapshot of a detailed assessment of selected, highly impacted, sectors. The study does not cover costs brought about by security-related issues.

The KRG Is Facing a Multifaceted Crisis Compounding Economic and Humanitarian Risks

Initially starting in early 2012 with the influx of Syrian refugees and later of IDPs in 2014, the situation has turned into a full-blown humanitarian crisis. At the beginning of 2015, there were 257,000 Syrian refugees and 1,003,300 Iraqi IDPs in the KRI. In addition, there were around 250,000 IDPs who came to the region before 2014. Therefore, in early 2015, the total number of refugees and IDPs added up to 1.5 million in KRI.[1] This constitutes a 28 percent increase in KRI's population. Of the total IDPs and refugees, 60 percent are in Dohuk. The large number of Iraqi IDPs and Syrian refugees reside in many of the same host communities, placing strains on the local economy and access to public services.[2] The impact and stabilization costs are high for the overall economy, as well as for social and infrastructure outcomes. This ESIA provides estimates of the shocks based on three scenarios. The baseline scenario's assumption is that the current population of Syrian refugees and IDPs will remain unchanged in 2015. Low and high cases with projected number of refugees are also provided for the purposes of sensitivity analysis. The low case scenario projects an additional influx of 30,000 Syrian refugees and 250,000 IDPs, and the high case scenario projects an additional influx of 100,000 Syrian refugees and 500,000 IDPs.

The combination of loss of fiscal transfers and the refugee and IDP crisis, which intensified most notably after mid-2014, have impacted all productive and social sectors, and their large and negative impacts are still unfolding. At the macroeconomic level it is estimated that the combined fiscal and refugee and IDP crises had depressed economic activity, and GDP growth declined from 8 percent in 2013 to 3 percent in 2014, a deceleration of 5 percentage points. This means that growth of wage incomes, profits, consumption, domestic and foreign investment, and local KRG revenues all slowed significantly. Prices have increased as has unemployment, and refugees and IDPs entering the labor market are pushing wages down. In terms of poverty, the ESIA estimates that KRI's poverty rate increased from 3.5 percent in 2012 up to 8.1 percent in 2014.[3] In terms of public finances, the crises resulted in sharply lower local revenues as well as increased borrowing from the private sector and quasi-fiscal deficits of about $3 billion (about 25 percent of fiscal transfer entitlement from the central government) to provide wages and salaries payments and to provide public services and goods, which included support for Syrian refugees and IDPs, albeit at much less quality and reduced access. This borrowing supported growth but at the cost of a rapid buildup of debt in a short period, which has implications for fiscal sustainability.

The study emphasizes that these effects are unfolding within a policy framework that has long-standing distortions. For example, electricity demand has sharply increased, but the government remains committed to provide fuel purchased from private refineries to private generators at a fixed price. The region's economy was already seeing supply-side strains from its dramatic growth before the crisis. Although socioeconomic outcomes in KRI are the best in Iraq, limitations exist in the delivery model for health, education, and infrastructure, which impeded investment and efficiency in these sectors. The study therefore elaborates on how these issues are affecting the government's ability to manage the crisis.

To Manage the Impact of These Shocks, KRG Will Need Additional Resources to Restore Access to Public Services

The headline finding of the report is that the overall stabilization cost from the inflow of refugees and IDPs is $1.4 billion for the baseline scenario for 2015. This cost is about 5.6 percent of nonoil GDP and thus in the range of costs observed for major disasters worldwide. The study analyzes the impacts of both shocks through a macrofiscal and sectoral approach. Table O.1 presents a stabilization assessment for nine sectors as well as aggregated needs to address human development and infrastructure issues. For 2015, low and high scenarios are also analyzed based on a possible additional influx of Syrian refugees and Iraqi IDPs. The study also finds significant, but difficult to quantify, indirect costs to households, including income losses from higher trade costs and job loss, along with generalized dilution of public good provision as a result of increased demand. A detailed impact assessment is presented in Appendix A.

TABLE 0.1
Stabilization Assessment, 2015 Projection
dollars, millions

	Baseline[a]		Low Scenario[b]		High Scenario[c]	
	Syrian Refugees	IDPs	Syrian Refugees	IDPs	Syrian Refugees	IDPs
Human Development						
Health	**70.4**	**246.7**	**81.3**	**336.1**	**107.0**	**425.5**
Recurrent spending	60.0	215.4	69.5	293.9	91.7	372.3
Primary health care	34.9	113.6	37.9	137.5	44.7	161.4
Hospital	25.1	101.8	31.7	156.3	46.9	210.9
Capital spending	10.3	31.3	11.8	42.3	15.3	53.1
Primary health care	9.5	28.2	10.9	38.0	14.2	47.7
Hospital	0.9	3.1	0.9	4.3	1.2	5.4
Education	**34.0**	**161.5**	**39.8**	**188.6**	**53.1**	**297.1**
Current spending	10.5	49.9	12.3	58.5	16.6	93.0
Teacher salaries	3.0	14.3	3.5	16.8	4.7	26.6
Books and school materials	7.5	35.6	8.8	41.8	11.8	66.4
Capital spending	23.5	111.6	27.4	130.1	36.5	204.1
School rehabilitation and additional caravans	23.5	111.6	27.4	130.1	36.5	204.1
Food Security and Agriculture	**34.3**	**121.1**	**39.4**	**162.0**	**51.1**	**203.0**
Recurrent spending						
Agricultural and livestock livelihood support	34.3	121.1	39.4	162.0	51.1	203.0
Poverty	**19.4**	**47.1**	**21.1**	**64.6**	**23.3**	**84.5**
Shelter	**111.3**		**10.0**	**194.6**	**33.3**	**277.9**
Total: Human Development	**845.9**		**1137.5**		**1555.7**	
Infrastructure						
Electricity	**64.8**	**210.0**	**79.7**	**283.9**	**114.6**	**402.6**
Current spending	60.2	188.1	68.9	210.1	89.2	276.7
Capital spending	4.6	21.9	10.8	73.9	25.4	125.9
Transport	**20.6**		**20.6**		**26.4**	
Capital spending						
Road maintenance expenditures	20.6		20.6		26.4	
Solid Waste Management	**5.9**	**20.0**	**6.7**	**26.9**	**8.7**	**33.7**
Current spending	3.5	12.0	4.0	16.1	5.2	20.2
Capital spending	2.3	8.0	2.7	10.8	3.5	13.5
Water	**51.8**	**162.5**	**58.5**	**216.7**	**75.9**	**271.8**
Current spending	46.3	140.3	52.1	186.7	67.6	234.2
Operations and maintenance needed for stabilization for out-camp	3.1	12.6	3.6	16.9	4.7	21.3
Provision of access of water and sanitation for in-camp	43.2	127.7	48.5	169.8	62.9	213.0
Capital spending	5.5	22.2	6.4	30.0	8.3	37.6
Capital investment needs for stabilization out-camp	5.5	22.2	6.4	30.0	8.3	37.6
Total: Infrastructure	**535.6**		**693.0**		**933.8**	
Grand Total: Human Development and Infrastructure	**1381.5**		**1830.4**		**2489.5**	

Note: IDPs = internally displaced persons.
a. Status quo—the current population of Syrian refugees and IDPs remains unchanged.
b. Additional influx of 30,000 Syrian refugees and 250,000 Iraqi IDPs.
c. Additional influx of 100,000 Syrian refugees and 500,000 Iraqi IDPs.

These Stabilization Assessment Findings and Main Channels of Impacts Are Subsequently Elaborated

The Syrian refugee and Iraqi IDP inflows into KRI had a pronounced impact on the economy. Moreover, the ISIS crisis happened in the context of an ongoing KRG budget crisis (since February 2014), and these three shocks hit the economy hard. The ISIS crisis presented a direct threat to KRI, adversely affecting trade routes. The fighting against ISIS has fragmented the local, national, and regional markets, undermining KRI's role as a safe base for and trade route to the larger southern Iraq market. Alternative routes for the movement of goods, services, and persons have been found but come at a cost. With public investment projects stalled, the construction sector has been particularly hard hit, with follow-on effects for other segments of the economy and the financial sector. The directness of the ISIS crisis worsened uncertainty in the investment climate in KRI and hence inhibited investment and growth.

Economic growth contracted 5 percentage points as a result of shocks. The initial channel for lower growth was the loss of revenue transfer from the central government in Iraq. KRG's share from the federal budget, 17 percent from the central government budget minus sovereign expenses, which corresponds to about $12 billion a year, or 80 percent of KRG's total revenues, has been withheld mainly because of the political gridlock in Baghdad, paralyzing the public sector since February 2014. The actual amount that has been transferred is about $1.1 billion to date. As a result, both revenues and expenditures registered large declines, and the government has accumulated large wages and salaries arrears. The execution of an investment budget has been put on hold, and many contractors have not been paid for a few months. The construction sector has been particularly affected, with small companies reporting bankruptcy. With the surge of ISIS activity midyear, the crisis moved to the economic and social sectors, putting further downward pressure on growth. Combined with declining public and private expenditure, aggregate demand continues to be restrained, and therefore GDP growth is expected to be considerably less than in 2013: Preliminary estimates show that the deceleration in 2014 will be about 5 percentage points relative to the previous baseline growth.

Given the loss of transfers, the Ministry of Natural Resources has been providing support to KRG, which avoided a collapse of the economy but at the cost of rapid buildup of debt in less than a year. The ministry assumed wages and salaries obligations by supporting the Ministry of Finance, albeit with lags. The ministry has borrowed about $1.5 billion from the domestic private sector and another $1.5 billion from international companies and suppliers by selling its future oil output. It also exported about $1.3 billion worth of oil. The ministry has been providing transfers for IDPs as well. The ministry estimates that about $1 billion was spent to provide the IDPs with basic support. In this way, the ministry injected about $5 billion, corresponding to 41 percent of the budgetary resources that were not transferred from the central government, into the economy, and this financial support avoided a total collapse of the economy. Had this support not materialized, economic growth would have been negative. Although this was a positive move, resources borrowed by the ministry are in essence quasi-fiscal activities of the public sector, which amounted to about 12 percent of regional GDP in 2014. These should be added to the budget deficits, for which 2014 end-year data are not yet available, which would mean that deficits for the year could be about 14–15 percent of GDP. Although KRG's debt stock is still low, because they are accumulating deficits at this rate, a 12 percent GDP point jump in debt in less than a year is a source of concern with implications for fiscal sustainability.

A surge in violence has led to supply-side shocks. Blocked transport routes and shortages in refined petroleum products as well as losses in investor confidence are affecting economic activities. ISIS-related impediments to public distribution system delivery led to temporary reductions in availability. Furthermore, KRG was obliged by the crisis to source from refineries much farther south, leading to an increase in the price of fuel—ranging from 14 percent in Sulaymaniyah to 15 percent in Erbil and 23 percent in Dohuk—and hence electricity and transport costs. Foreign direct investment flows have declined, and operations of foreign enterprises have been adversely affected. The crisis has had a direct effect on all investment, which has declined by two-thirds so far in 2014. For example, Erbil Steel, which produced 18,000 tons of steel bars every month, evacuated its workers in June and closed its facility. Another example is the cement sector, which has stopped supplying the southern market for several months.

The ISIS crisis has had a significant effect on trade of goods and services. KRI's role as a transit trade route to southern Iraq was severely affected. Between May and July 2014, Iraq's exports declined by about 25 percent and its imports by 45 percent. Turkish exports to Iraq decreased by one-third to $1.3 billion in June and July. Services exports have declined because of reduced transit trade and reduced tourism. The number of trucks entering through the Ibrahim Khalil customs post with Turkey has declined from more than 3,000 per day to about 600 per day. The ISIS crisis has also led to a dramatic reduction in tourism: Tourist inflows, which had increased by 33 percent in 2013 to nearly 3 million, are reported to have declined to fewer than 800,000 in the first six months of 2014.

The Refugee and IDP Crises Have Imposed Substantial Strains on the Social Sectors, and Additional Resources Are Needed to Address Humanitarian Issues

Stabilizing the combined effects of the Syrian refugee crisis and the arrival of IDPs in sectors related to human development, including health, education, social safety nets, and food security, will require about $846 million (3.5 percent of GDP) in 2015. The growing inflow of Syrian refugees and internally displaced Iraqis into KRI in 2012–2014 has put significant pressures on the regional government and severely constrained the delivery of health, education, and social protection programs to the population. The standard of living has deteriorated, and a noticeable proportion of the population has fallen into poverty or is vulnerable to falling into poverty.

Poverty is increasing, and social protection programs need support. The crises in Iraq and Syria have had a profound effect on the welfare of the people in KRI. As a result of the multiple crises, the poverty rate for KRI more than doubled, from 3.8 percent at the natural population growth rate in 2014 to 8.1 percent. A rough estimate of the amount of resources necessary on average to bring poverty rates down to the "without-crisis" level are estimated to range from $66.5 million to $107.8 million for 2015. Social protection programs need to be strengthened to mitigate the impact on the livelihoods of the population. The federal government had started the implementation of a new Social Protection Law, which stipulated an increase in the social allowance to reach on average ID 420,000 per household monthly. The Kurdish households that would fall below the poverty line will be eligible to receive social safety net cash transfers. The Ministry of Labor and Social Affairs (MOLSA), the main KRG agency charged with providing social safety net assistance in KRI, manages the cash-transfer social safety net program. This program provides cash transfers to specific groups considered vulnerable.

Food security for KRI is hampered by the disruption of transportation routes. The governorates most affected by the ISIS crisis, Nineveh and Salahaddin, on average contribute nearly a third of Iraq's wheat production and about 38 percent of its barley. Many grain silos, some of which serve KRI populations, have been captured by insurgents. Increased food demand in KRI caused by the increased population is being met fully by food imports. Domestic agriculture, already in decline, has been further disrupted by decreased government contracts. The cost of the public distribution system (PDS), agricultural budget support to farmers, as well as food assistance to refugees and IDPs continue to dominate government expenditures. Although food security in KRI has been sustained during the Syrian refugee influx, the recent IDP surge is resulting in food insecurity. The PDS for subsidizing food staples, although operational, is not functioning optimally. Thus host communities, especially vulnerable groups within them, are also being directly impacted. The estimate for ensuring sufficient food supplies is $155.4 million under the baseline scenario for 2015.

An immediate need is seen for housing and shelter in KRI. Adequate shelter needs to be provided immediately to more than 243,000 vulnerable IDPs. Providing adequate shelter for such a large population has proven an immense challenge for both KRG and the international humanitarian community. The government has built 26 IDP camps across the three KRI governorates with a total combined capacity for hosting 223,790 IDPs. KRG has committed to funding three out of these 26 camps, and the international community is expected to fund 20 camps, with the remaining three camps remaining unfunded.[4] The stabilization costs for sheltering the IDPs are estimated at $111.3 million.[5]

The crises have led to a major increase in demand in the health sector, and in the absence of a budget increase the current burden of disease and other health outcomes are likely to be negatively impacted. Between October 2012 and September 2014, because of increased population, the host communities in KRI have been deprived of health spending, with implications for overall health system performance. Although external donors have tried to support KRG, a significant amount of financial resources is still required to restore stability to the health sector, while maintaining the host community's precrisis access levels. On the basis of findings from field site visits to refugee and IDP camps, it is evident that the displaced people are at a high risk of developing disease as a result of increased exposure to numerous environmental factors (for example, poor water and sanitation facilities), as well as increased nutrition vulnerability. In light of this, higher utilization levels of both PHC and hospital services would be expected. It is estimated that the health sector will need an additional $317 million to stabilize the situation.

The crisis has pushed the capacity of the KRI education system to its limits. It is estimated that 325,000 of the Syrian refugees and Iraqi IDPs are children younger than 18 years of age. Most school-aged children remain largely out of the education system in KRI. Among school-aged children, 70 percent of IDPs and 48 percent of refugees are not enrolled in school. Although immediate priorities are related to infrastructure (e.g., school renovation, classroom expansion and construction), it is equally important to make sure that teachers are deployed and paid, text-books are provided, language barriers are addressed, and the security and safety of children are insured. It is also important for the refugees and IDPs to be made aware of the educational opportunities, where available, and that access is improved. It is estimated that, under the baseline scenario, KRG will need about $34.0 million for refugees and $161.5 million for IDPs to stabilize the education sector.

The Crisis Increased the Stress on Infrastructure, Including Water, Solid Waste Management, Electricity, and Transport Sectors: The Stabilization Cost Is Enormous

The crises have had an impact on domestic energy demand and prices. Gasoline prices increased to ID 900/liter, and the price for diesel doubled to ID 950/liter in June 2014. These sharp increases have impacted economic activities. The electricity sector is heavily dependent on government support. The Ministry of Finance transferred ID 80 billion each month in 2013. The tariff level and collection rates are insufficient to cover operating costs and capital expenditures. Demand is increasing: For example, the electricity network demand load in Erbil reached its peak in August 2014 through a 22 percent increase compared with August 2013. In Sulaymaniyah, an additional capacity of 125 MW is needed. Notwithstanding the considerable infrastructure development in recent years, systemic problems remain. The stabilization cost for 2015 is estimated to range between $275 million and $517 million across the baseline and high-case scenarios.

Water demand is increasing in KRI, and the sanitation situation is a concern, especially in the camps. Water supply and sanitation systems were already facing challenges before the crisis. Between October 2012 and September 2014, the additional demand for water for refugees and IDPs is estimated at 11 percent, which put further pressure on the water supply. The sharp increase in water demand has not been accompanied by investments in wastewater infrastructure. As a result of the crisis, KRG now needs to meet an additional estimated total water demand of 17.1 million square meters per year. The sanitation situation is a concern, and the major gaps for the sewerage sector relate to the lack of physical facilities: no wastewater treatment plants and no sewage collection networks except in the Sulaymaniyah Governorate. Because of the current lack of wastewater treatment plants in KRI, the wastewater is directly discharged into rivers. It is estimated that stabilization needs in this sector will be about $214.3 million in 2015.

PHOTO 0.1
Children in Arbat Camp in Sulaymaniyah Governorate

Refugee and IDP children running behind a truck loaded with boxes containing clothes donated from international partners, September 2014. IDP = internally displaced person. © Sibel Kulaksiz. Used with the permission of Sibel Kulaksiz; further permission required for reuse.

The crisis is adding stress on an already existing ailing system of solid waste management. An average of 2.5 to 3.5 kilograms of solid waste was generated by in-camp refugees and IDPs and 1.2 kilograms by IDPs and refugees living in regular housing dwellings. This additional population produced more than 1,690 tons of solid waste per day, an increase of 26 percent on KRI's daily per capita generated solid waste in 2014. In terms of capacity for absorbing solid waste, it appears that only Dohuk City is ready to continue to accept additional solid waste because of the construction of a new sanitary landfill, and because of its current capacity for recycling. It is expected that beginning in 2015, the following interventions in solid waste management in KRI would be required: (1) the closure and rehabilitation of open and uncontrolled municipal solid waste dumps, especially in Erbil and Sulaymaniyah; (2) establishing composting, separating, and landfilling facilities, especially in Erbil, which has no waste recycling activities; and (3) locating appropriate land and construction of a new sanitary landfill to serve Sulaymaniyah City and surroundings.

The combination of the crisis and influx of IDPs and indirectly the Syrian refugees have caused an increase in the wear and tear on the road network and have damaged several bridges and sections of road. The crisis has resulted in the closure of one of the main trade routes between north and south from Dohuk to Erbil via Mosul. The IDPs who fled their homes using their own vehicles caused an abrupt increase in traffic by about 20 percent. The humanitarian relief efforts, including heavy supply trucks carrying food, medicine, and construction material (more so than the Syrian refugees themselves, who are mostly lower income and primarily housed in shelters outside the major cities in Dohuk), have also added a toll on the road network. All these factors have contributed to the increase in congestion, travel time, traffic accidents, and local road network wear and tear. The crisis, primarily the fighting with ISIS, has also had severe impacts on parts of the network, especially that at the frontier at the borders with Syrian borders as well as Mosul governorate. Already eight bridges in the three governorates (Erbil, Dohuk, and Sulaymaniyah) have either been fully or partially destroyed by recent military conflict. The crisis has also taken a toll on the internal municipal road network.

The influx of IDPs and refugees will also have environmental impacts. Immediate environmental concerns include those that have a direct impact on human health in both displaced and host communities, such as incidences of low-quality potable water both inside and outside camps; increases in raw, undirected sewage outflows, because KRI has no wastewater treatment infrastructure in place; and increased solid waste dumping without concurrent increases in water pickup and proper disposal. With the arrival of winter, increased demand for cooking and heating fuel may lead to increases in illegal firewood harvesting as well as in health impacts of indoor air pollution, especially on children and the aged. The capacity of primary infrastructural resources, such as power and transport, will be stretched to their capacities, resulting in high air pollution loads as well.

Conclusions

This ESIA provides a technical assessment of the impact of the crises and stabilization needs that could inform the dialogue between the regional and central governments as well as provide input for international efforts to address socioeconomic issues. The crisis calls for numerous actions moving forward. In the short term, many of the solutions for averting the humanitarian crisis are beyond KRG's control and require national and international responses. Should the refugees and IDPs remain in KRI, this ESIA could be used as a gauge of the financial resources needed (in addition to KRG's share from the annual budget) to address the needs of the displaced people and host communities. Furthermore, the findings for stabilization needs of specific sectors could be used to inform KRG's budget allocation decisions.

In the medium term, structural reforms are required. Although it is a priority to provide necessary relief to deal with economic and social issues caused by the crisis, it is also important for the government to develop longer-term strategies to address structural development issues. Refugees and IDPs are likely to remain in KRI for an extended period, and so they will be seeking employment opportunities. The recent crisis has highlighted the strong dependence and vulnerability of KRG on transfers from the central Iraqi government and insufficient direct contribution of other sectors to KRI's economy. KRG has already recognized the need for the diversification of the economy. According to the 2020 KRG Vision, with proven natural resources and labor force, KRG has the potential to accelerate economic growth. One of the main pillars of the KRG Vision is the development of a diversified economy driven by the private sector. A dynamic private sector would provide job opportunities to the KRI population, as well as to the refugees and IDPs. The World Bank's upcoming growth diagnostics study will be a tool to refine and implement this vision and will propose specific policies.

Notes

1. The refugee and IDP numbers are obtained from the KRG Ministry of Planning; and from the KRG and United Nations' *Immediate Response Plan Phase II (IRP2) for Internally Displaced People in the Kurdistan Region of Iraq.*
2. In December 2014, there were 2,350,000 overall displaced people in Iraq.
3. This is assuming that not all refugees and IDPs are poor.
4. The 2012 SEINA report and the KRG Immediate Response Plan.
5. This is based on the assumption of a cost of providing shelter of $833 per person. This does not include the cost of providing security for camps. Costs inevitably are associated with the securitization of camps, but that concern is beyond the scope of this assessment.

Introduction

The Kurdistan Region of the Republic of Iraq (KRI) is a constitutionally recognized semiautonomous region in northern Iraq with a population of 5.1 million (2012 estimate).[1] Its government (the KRG), based in Erbil, has the right—under the Iraqi constitution of 2005—to exercise legislative, executive, and judicial powers according to the constitution, except in what is listed therein as exclusive powers of the federal authorities.

KRG is facing a multifaceted and complex crisis compounding concurrent and mutually aggravating security, political, economic, and social risks. The Islamic State in Iraq and Syria (ISIS) crisis has significantly undermined the population's well-being and the authorities' ability to respond to the humanitarian crisis since the summer of 2014. A key priority of KRG has thus been to bolster internal and external security, diverting an increasing share of public finance toward defense and security spending. In addition to the impact of the Syrian and ISIS crises, which are the focus of this study, a third shock took place: The central government in Baghdad failed to pass a budget in 2014 and did not make the agreed fiscal transfers to KRG, contracting the region's fiscal space. These transfers amount to nearly half of KRG's gross domestic product (GDP), and so isolating the effect of the Syrian and ISIS crises from the budgetary crisis presents a special challenge for the current exercise.

The scale and acceleration of the displacement crisis took KRG by surprise. The United Nations (UN) and other humanitarian agencies have made tremendous efforts to address the immense needs of the displaced. KRG, the private sector, and local residents were also quick to mobilize both financial and in-kind donations for those in needs. However, multiple competing emergencies requiring international assistance in combination with the shortage of local funds due to the lack of fiscal transfers from Baghdad are threatening the future delivery of even basic services. In addition, the capacity of both the international humanitarian community and KRG is being stretched to the limit, which would also hamper the future response to the crisis should the financing constraints be softened.

The overriding need to address the immediate humanitarian emergency has left little time or capacity to prepare for the medium term and mitigate any long-term development impact. The impact of the current displacement crisis goes beyond the financial cost of covering the urgent needs of the refugees and internally displaced persons (IDPs). A significant population increase over such a short period not only will cause unsustainable strain on existing services and infrastructure, but also can cause long-term distortions, for example, in the labor and housing market, and might impact the social fabric and cohesion of the population. To minimize longer term adverse impact, it is important that the cost of hosting such a large vulnerable population does not disproportionally fall on citizens of KRI.

Refugees who have settled outside camps are finding it hard to find the necessary resources to cover their basic needs. According to a September 2014 comparative analysis of camp and noncamp refugee populations completed by the United Nations High Commissioner for Refugees (UNHCR), 95 percent of refugees in camps reported being able to afford the cost of meeting their basic needs,[2] as opposed to 70 percent outside camps. Part of this disparity may be attributed to the large number of IDPs who now reside in many of the same host communities as Syrian refugees (particularly in Dohuk Governorate), placing strains on these hosts and the preexisting population of Syrian refugees living on the local economy.

With regard to recent IDP inflow, displacement into the KRI proceeded in three distinct phases over 2014. Beginning in January, intense fighting in Fallujah and Ramadi forced population movements from these cities and into surrounding areas, Baghdad, and KRI. A second wave of IDPs entered KRI in June and July 2014 after ISIS took control of Mosul and fighting spread across Ninewa and Salah al Din governorates. A third phase took place in August when large numbers of residents in the Sinjar area fled heavy fighting between ISIS and Peshmerga (the KRI military forces). A saturated absorptive capacity of the housing market and lack of financial resources have left many persons without adequate shelter, leaving families to find cover in public buildings such as schools, or in the open covered only by unfinished construction projects or bridges.

Throughout this Economic and Social Impact Assessment (ESIA) report, a common methodology is followed. First, the report provides a baseline of the specific sector before the conflict, along with its performance during the conflict. The "impact assessment" is measured as the difference between (1) the actual out-turn (spending) for the variable of interest in period *t* and (2) the spending that would have occurred in period *t* had the conflict not occurred (counterfactual). Then the "stabilization assessment" measures spending needed in period *t* to maintain the preconflict level of access to and quality of public services. A detailed methodology is presented in Appendix B. The report uses a mixture of bottom-up and top-down approaches. In the bottom-up approach, sector teams with expertise in human development and infrastructure conducted sectoral assessments of crisis effects. In the top-down approach, available information on the national accounts, budget, trade flows, and current socioeconomic conditions was used where possible. Quantitative data are limited at the regional level, and so the quantitative methodology is complemented by a qualitative approach. Furthermore, in addition to on-budget data (for both current and capital budget), off-budget spending is taken into consideration, that is, spending by UN and other international/bilateral partners for specific sectors. The effect of the budget crisis is separated from other issues in the methodology—the Syrian civil war and ISIS, which are the focus of this report. The findings were controlled for the reductions in budget transfers. Also, in addition to direct costs, "hidden" and indirect costs are analyzed.

Three scenarios are analyzed in this ESIA report. Data for 2010 and 2011 are actuals, and 2011 is the base year of the assessment. Findings for 2012, 2013, 2014, and 2015 show the impact and stabilization assessment of Syrian refugees. In contrast, years 2014 and 2015 show the impact and stabilization assessment of Iraqi IDPs. Therefore, 2014 and 2015 projections present the combined impact of Syrian refugees and Iraqi IDPs. The impact of Syrian refugees and Iraqi IDPs are disintegrated for all sectors. Projections for 2015 projections include three scenarios: (1) baseline: status quo, namely, the current population of Syrian refugees and IDPs remains unchanged; (2) lower bound: a moderate (additional) increase in refugees and IDPs, namely, an additional 250,000 IDPs and 30,000 additional refugees; and (3) upper bound: a significant increase in both refugee and IDP inflows, namely, an additional 500,000 IDPs and an anticipated 100,000 refugees.

Data caveats are significant for an analytical work at the subregional level. The absence of reliable data at the regional level makes a meaningful analysis difficult. Although a significant amount of data was collected during the technical mission in full partnership with KRG authorities, the lack of detailed time series and macrostatistics creates challenges for in-depth analytical work. Therefore, the team relied on qualitative assessments in addition to quantitative calculations. KRG could benefit from targeted technical assistance on data development.

This ESIA report is organized in three chapters: (1) the macrofiscal impact of the crises, (2) the social development impact of the crises, and

(3) the infrastructure impact of the crises. Under the macrofiscal impact of the crises, macroeconomic and fiscal implications are analyzed with a focus impact on trade in goods and services, the private sector, and financial services. The social development impact of the crises identified impact and stabilization costs in the health and education sectors, as well as for food security and agricultural livelihood, poverty and welfare, social assistance and labor, housing and shelter, and social cohesion and citizen security. The final chapter on the impact of the conflicts on infrastructure focuses on water and sanitation, solid waste management, and the energy and transportation sectors.

Notes

1. Iraq's overall population (including KRG) was estimated at 34 million in 2012.
2. Basic needs include food, water, fuel, transport, clothing, hygiene items, health care, education, and rent.

CHAPTER 1

Macroeconomic and Fiscal Impact of the Conflict

The Syrian refugee inflows since 2012, the fighting against ISIS in 2014, and the subsequent Iraqi population movements into KRI had a pronounced impact on the economy. Moreover, the ISIS crisis happened in the context of an ongoing KRG budget crisis (since February 2014), and these three shocks hit the economy hard. The ISIS crisis presented a direct threat to KRI, adversely affecting trade routes. Fighting against the group has fragmented local, national, and regional markets, undermining KRI's role as a safe base for and trade route to the larger southern Iraq market. Alternative routes for the movement of goods, services, and persons have been found but come at a cost. With public investment projects stalled, the construction sector has particularly been hit hard, with follow-on effects for other segments of the economy and the financial sector. The directness of the ISIS crisis worsened uncertainty in the KRI investment climate and hence inhibited investment and growth.

Economic growth declined relative to the previous baseline in 2014 as a result of multiple shocks. With public and private expenditure disbursements down almost 60 percent, aggregate demand continues to be restrained, with negative impact on growth. Projections show that the economy's growth rate was about 3 percent in 2014 compared with a previous baseline of 8 percent growth. A GDP growth rate of 3 percent mainly reflects private sector activities during the first half of the year and financial support of the Ministry of Natural Resources to the government. In 2014 the actual fiscal transfer from the Iraqi central government to KRG is about $1.1 billion. In addition, the Ministry of Natural Resources has borrowed about $1.5 billion from the domestic private sector and another $1.5 billion from international companies and suppliers by selling its future oil output. It also exported about $1.3 billion worth of oil.

The ministry has been providing wages and salaries payments—except for a couple of months in 2014—as well as transfers for refugees and IDPs. It is estimated that the ministry incurred about $1 billion to provide the IDPs with basic support.

The spending impact has been high for public and private sectors and for households. In 2014, because of the ongoing security and budget crises, the performance of governmental contracts was negatively affected. Compensation for late payments is expected to cost an additional ID 244.4 billion ($209.6 million) in the 2015 budget. A welfare impact is seen for the host community as a result of IDP inflows. The simulated impact of IDPs' arrival on the monetary well-being of KRI residents is projected to be about $910 million in 2014. Furthermore, welfare costs for KRI citizens as a consequence of the increase in trade costs are crudely estimated to be an annualized amount of $561 million.

In the medium to longer term, the refugee and IDP crises are likely to bring a more profound challenge to the economy. The threat of widening conflict and the climate of uncertainty could further inhibit trade and investment. The security deterioration might affect more severely investors that were considering entering the KRI/Iraq market. For example, a half dozen new international five-star hotels were set to begin operations in Erbil in the next two to three years. These investments are likely to be postponed as a result of the ISIS crisis. In the case of a prolonged conflict, it is likely that refugee and IDP inflows will further increase, and the displaced will need income-generating opportunities. Opportunities will have to be created, largely in the private sector. Having lost most of their assets and having used most of their savings for their immediate needs, the displaced will need access to finance to establish themselves as entrepreneurs.

Precrises Macroeconomic Situation

Output

The relatively stable security environment has allowed economic progress in KRI before 2014. After achieving a semiautonomous status in 2005, KRI's economy expanded every year, and its real economic growth rate was about 8 percent in 2013 (Invest In Group – KRG Department of Foreign Relations 2014), driven primarily by oil production. In the past few years, the construction sector has been an important source of growth followed by agriculture and services. These relatively high economic growth rates have been supported by large public spending, especially by large capital spending. Figure 1.1 shows that nominal GDP increased

FIGURE 1.1
KRI GDP at Current Prices, 2004–11
ID, billions

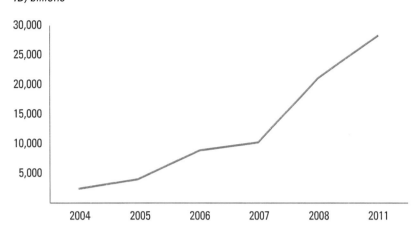

Source: KRSO.

from ID 20,954 billion in 2008 to ID 28,320 billion in 2011.[1] Per capita nominal GDP was $4,452 for KRI in 2011, recording an increase of 12.1 percent between 2008 and 2011.

The oil sector is the main source of economic growth. Market sources estimated KRI oil production at 250,000 barrels a day in 2013.[2] According to the International Energy Agency, oil production in KRI will increase to 500,000–800,000 barrels per day by 2020, and to between 750,000 barrels and 1.2 million barrels a day by 2035. There are 47 international oil companies from 17 countries operating in KRI. The international oil companies have committed to invest approximately $10 billion in the energy sector.

Public Finances

KRG's budgetary resources heavily depend on transfers from the central Iraqi government. According to the Iraq Budget Law, KRG is to receive 17 percent from the central budget minus sovereign expenses. These resources represent about 80 percent of its annual budget revenues (about 50 percent of its GDP), supplemented by oil exports, taxes, and fees collected locally (table 1.1). In March 2013, Iraq's cabinet approved a budget of 138 trillion Iraqi dinars ($118.6 billion) based on a world oil price of $90 per barrel and expected oil exports of 2.9 million barrels per day, allocating some $650 million to central government payments to companies working in KRI in addition to the 17 percent share KRG receives from the national budget. However, KRG had originally requested

TABLE 1.1
Revenue and Expenditures, 2010–14
ID, millions

	Budget					Actual				
	2010	2011	2012	2013	2014	2010	2011	2012	2013	June 30, 2014
Revenue										
Region's share of the federal budget, Iraq	10,143,871	11,484,468	12,604,950	14,406,735	0	10,252,856	11,289,100	12,559,824	14,288,706	1,114,000
Taxes	196,605	276,811	236,134	183,107	0	447,044	559,025	716,346	773,636	532,795
Social benefits (nontaxes)	0	0	0	0	0	97	80,316	202,257	161,069	0
Revenue from oil sales	0	0	0	0	0	0	0	0	0	0
Grants	0	0	0	0	0	0	0	0	0	0
Other revenue	152,074	624,425	259,866	668,007	0	295,325	492,536	1,616,405	2,477,604	1,303,885
Deposit	0	0	0	0	0	374,305	149,718	583,735	645,143	885,105
Total revenue	**10,492,550**	**12,385,704**	**13,200,950**	**15,257,849**	**0**	**11,369,627**	**12,570,695**	**15,678,567**	**18,346,158**	**3,835,785**
Expenditures										
Basic salaries and wages	3,558,825	4,876,375	6,450,975	5,869,222	0	4,342,832	5,762,056	6,886,249	7,603,439	3,613,068
Social security contributions	2,599,114	2,714,914	2,991,986	3,780,319	0	2,495,013	2,625,599	2,673,038	3,519,407	1,197,488
Interest payments	0	0	0	0	0	0	0	0	0	0
Goods, services, maintenance	1,082,821	1,659,381	3,016,988	2,337,030	0	1,947,831	3,758,753	3,899,208	3,738,296	1,594,094
Investment expenses	3,251,790	4,700,000	4,720,000	5,343,791	0	1,783,902	2,243,819	3,267,999	3,839,620	1,595,030
Total expenditures	**10,492,550**	**13,950,670**	**17,179,949**	**17,330,362**	**0**	**10,569,578**	**14,390,227**	**16,672,494**	**18,700,762**	**7,999,680**
Balance	**0**	**(1,564,966)**	**(3,978,999)**	**2,072,513**	**0**	**(1,011,603)**	**(211,554)**	**(2,031,086)**	**(3,025,013)**	**(3,379,617)**
Primary fiscal balance	**0**	**0**	**0**	**0**	**0**	**(211,554)**	**2,031,086**	**(3,025,013)**	**(3,379,617)**	**(7,543,512)**
Memo: Defense expenditures	1,957,000	2,078,382	3,123,030	3,539,393	0	2,725,794	3,284,089	3,869,462	4,226,051	0

Source: KRG Ministry of Finance and Economy.

an additional budget allocation of about $3.5 billion, which it claimed included the outstanding payments of all oil and gas exports between 2010 and 2013.

KRG's budget deficits have averaged about 1–2 percent of estimated GDP and have been mostly financed by domestic borrowing, although some of the operations of the Ministry of Natural Resources involve quasi-fiscal activities. Hence, actual public sector spending is higher than the budget data show. Although the 2014 ministry financial report is not available yet, the 2013 financial report shows that projects worth about $3.2 billion were funded by the ministry, corresponding to about 1.6 percent of GDP. Combined with the capital spending figures reported below, estimated KRG total public sector spending was about 4–5 percent of regional GDP in 2013.

External and domestic borrowing by the Ministry of Natural Resources avoided a total collapse of the economy, but this raises concerns about the sustainability of public finances. The ministry borrowed about $3 billion and exported oil valued at $1.3 millon, accounting for roughly 41 percent of its budgetary oil revenue entitlement or 12 percent of GDP, and spent these resources domestically, which supported growth. As a result, the real fiscal deficit jumped by about 12 percent of GDP from an almost zero external debt position over the course of one year. The buildup of debt, although the external debt stock is still low, at such a rapid pace warrants the attention of the authorities.

Moreover, a review of budgetary and other expenditures would inform KRG about reform options in the area of public finance. KRG's wages and salaries costs are very high and the most rapidly growing budget item. In 2013 KRG allocated 36.6 percent of budget to wages and salaries. Furthermore, social benefits, pensions, and subsidies form a large share of the KRG budget. Indeed, the economic composition of public expenditure for KRG shows that social benefits, pensions, and subsidies together accounted for 13.9 percent of total budget allocation in 2013 (figure 1.2). Iraq's social protection system goes beyond the "ration card." The KRG budget spends each year about $2.4 billion to subsidize electricity, the water supply, and agriculture. A more efficient, prioritized, and effective delivery of these benefits is required, which could be determined by undertaking a Public Expenditure Review.

Despite high growth in capital budget allocation in recent years, infrastructure gaps remain in KRI. In 2013, of KRG's approved budget, more than 37 percent was to be spent on capital investment. Public contracting in KRI is a major component of the national economy, cutting across nearly every area of planning, program management, and budgeting. In addition to the capital investment budget, one finds provincial developments plus other budgets allocated for public investment projects.

FIGURE 1.2
KRG Economic Composition of Public Expenditures, 2013
percentage share in KRG budget allocation

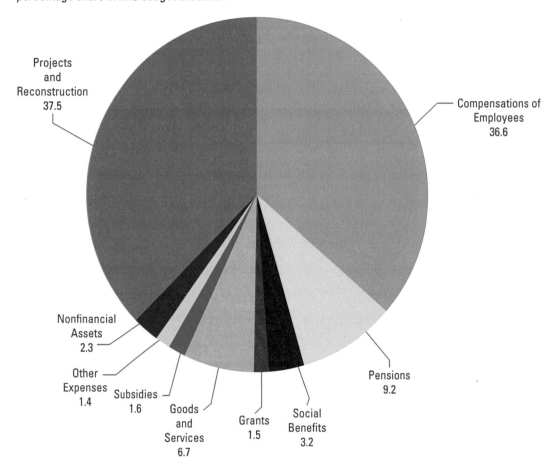

Projects and Reconstruction 37.5

Compensations of Employees 36.6

Nonfinancial Assets 2.3

Other Expenses 1.4

Subsidies 1.6

Goods and Services 6.7

Grants 1.5

Social Benefits 3.2

Pensions 9.2

However, significant infrastructure gaps remain in the region, especially after the ISIS crisis. The government prioritizes water, sanitation, and environment sectors for public investment.

Investment and Private Sector Activities

The KRI private sector is relatively small and underdeveloped. The private sector grew, but from a low base, and the financial sector remained largely underdeveloped. Starting from a low base, registration of private sector firms has increased significantly in KRI, especially in Erbil Governorate. The number of KRI registered firms has grown from 7,440 in 2008 to 13,216 in 2011 and to 20,994 in July 2014. Most of these firms are local firms; of 20,994 registered firms, only 2,822 are foreign firms.

The private sector is concentrated in Erbil Governorate, where 63 percent of local firms and 74 percent of foreign firms are registered (figure 1.3).

KRI is seen by large firms as the secure gateway to the 30 million inhabitant market in the rest of Iraq. The main reason for KRI being a preferred location for investments is its strategic location within Iraq, its better security and political stability situation, and its friendlier business climate compared with that of Iraq (table 1.2). Although overall KRI outperforms Iraq in terms of business climate, its performance is mixed: It performs better on taxes, market opportunities, foreign direct investment policy, and macroeconomic environment. KRG's Investment Law (2006), offering tax and customs exemptions, in particular is considered very attractive. For instance, it provides for exemption from all noncustom

FIGURE 1.3
Number of Local and Foreign Registered Firms: Erbil, Sulaymaniyah, and Dohuk Governorates, 2008–14

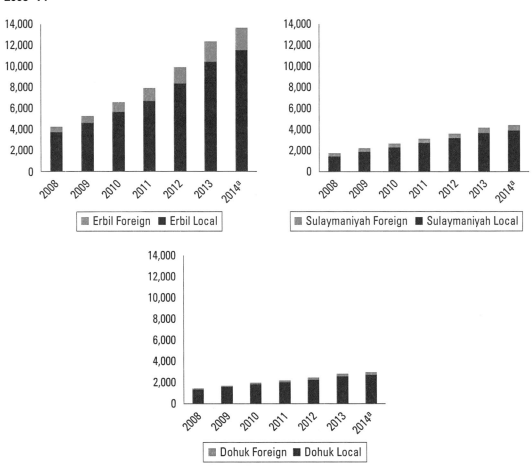

Source: KRG Board of Investment.
a. Until July 2014.

TABLE 1.2
Comparative Indexes, KRI versus Iraq

Ranking (absolute number)	KRI	Iraq
Global Peace Index	115th (2.25)	160th (3.38)
Security and Political Stability Index	83rd (41.0)	177th (86.5)
Political Environment Index	55th (4.98)	83rd (2.21)
Business Environment Index	57th (5.70)	72nd (5.04)

Sources: Institute for Economics and Peace; *The Economist* Business Intelligence Unit.

taxes and duties for 10 years starting from the date of providing services by the project or the date of actual production. However, KRI performs more poorly than Iraq on the labor market, financing conditions, and infrastructure.

KRG-licensed investment projects between November 2006 and September 7, 2014, amounted to an estimated $41.2 billion in capital (figure 1.4), including local investment, foreign direct investment, and joint ventures. These reported capital investments are projections at the time of licensing. Project progress is monitored by the Board of Investment on a regular basis. However, no detailed data on actual investments are available. The year 2013 saw peak investments of $12.4 billion, including a few exceptionally large investments: $1.2 billion for a power plant by an Iraqi investor; another $1 billion for a power plant by an Iraqi investor; $2 billion for Arbet industrial city by an Iraq–Islamic Republic of Iran joint venture; and $2.4 billion for Eemar downtown by a United Arab Emirates investor. During the first nine months of 2014, projects with investment capital of $4.2 billion were licensed. The number of investments registered is likely to go down for the remaining months of the year as a result of the crises and is thus likely to remain below $5.6 billion.

Foreign investments and joint ventures accounted for 23.2 percent of the total investment since 2006. KRI succeeded in attracting both foreign and local private investors. Erbil Governorate has been particularly successful in attracting foreign investors, whereas Sulaymaniyah Governorate has the most joint ventures. Investments from the United Arab Emirates (including joint ventures) accounted for 7.1 percent of total investment between 2006 and 2014. Other major investors were from the Arab Republic of Egypt, Canada, the Islamic Republic of Iran, Lebanon, Spain, Turkey, the United Kingdom, and the United States. Investments from Turkey to KRI (including foreign investment and joint ventures) went up

FIGURE 1.4
KRI-Licensed Investment Project Capital, 2006–14
dollars, millions

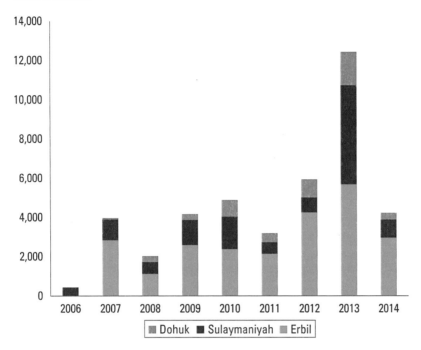

Source: KRG Board of Investment.

from $113.8 million in 2011 to $317.4 million in 2013; however, the year 2014 (as of September 7) is seeing hardly any Turkish investments.

In the period since 2011, the base year for the ESIA, the KRI economy was growing across a range of sectors. The main sectors that attracted investment are housing, industry, tourism, and trade (figure 1.5). The KRG Board of Investment initially awarded more than half of all investment licenses to housing projects, although the lack of a clear sector strategy and speculation in housing properties prompted the board to freeze all new investment licenses issued in the sector by mid-2012.

As of July 2014, KRI's installed plants are largely represented in the construction sector (35 percent) and metals sector (27 percent) (figure 1.6). Of installed plants, 58 percent are located in Erbil Governorate, 27 percent in Sulaymaniyah Governorate, and 15 percent in Dohuk Governorate. The number of annually installed plants has increased from 172 in 2011 to 594 in 2013. The year 2013 was a peak year, especially for Erbil Governorate, with 426 installed plants in Erbil Governorate alone. However, in the first seven months of 2014 only 36 newly installed plants were reported to the Ministry of Trade and Industry.

Tourism was a growing sector. In 2013 KRI tourism revenues amounted to an estimated $1 billion. More than 250 hotels are found in

FIGURE 1.5

KRI Investment, by Sector, November 2006 through September 7, 2014

dollars, millions

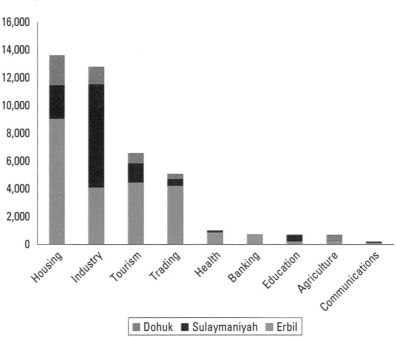

Source: KRG Board of Investment.

Erbil alone, out of which an estimated 60 hotels are in the two to five star range. Hotel occupancy rates in 2013 were reportedly at 75 percent, and about 3 million tourists visited KRI in 2013.

KRI plays an important role as a transit trade route to the rest of Iraq. Volumes of imports have continued to increase in 2009–13; however, KRI's imports out of Iraq's total imports have declined from 49 to 45 percent. Turkey is a large exporter to Iraq, and about two-thirds of Turkey's exports to Iraq (68 percent in 2013) go to KRI (figure 1.7).

Financial Sector

KRI is characterized by a low level of development of the financial sector. In KRI the banking sector consists of three state-owned banks, 19 local private banks, 11 foreign private banks, and six local and one foreign Islamic banks. One microfinance institution (MFI; Bright Futures Foundation) is focused specifically on KRI, and various larger MFIs have operations in KRI (Al Aman, Al Thiqa, CHF, Izdiharuna, Relief International). As of end 2013, KRI outreach was estimated to be approximately 15,198 loans outstanding valued at $29 million, representing

FIGURE 1.6
Installed Plants in Industry Sector, July 2014
percent

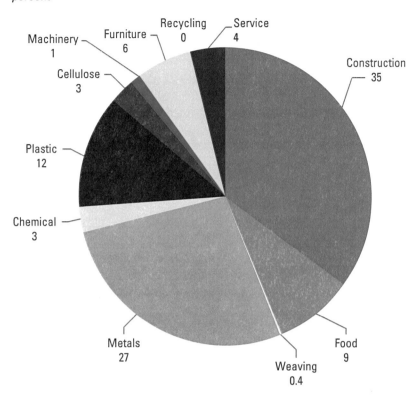

FIGURE 1.7
Imports from the World and Turkey to KRI, 2009–13
dollars, millions

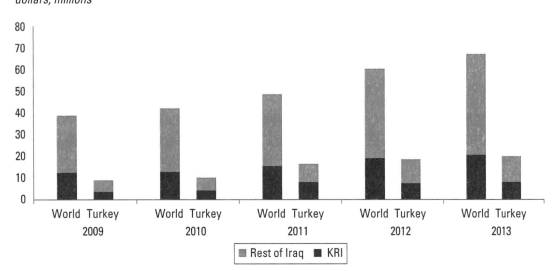

20 percent of the overall market share (based on percentage share of outstanding loans).

A general distrust in the banking sector is found because of decades of financial sector instability, with loss of deposits uncompensated. This has led to a strong preference for cash that continues, and salary payments (for both civil servants and private sector employees) are often made in cash, rather than through commercial banks. The 2011 Enterprise Survey for Iraq confirms that few firms rely on the banking sector. Of firms in Erbil and Sulaymaniyah, 3.2 percent and 3.1 percent, respectively, report that they have a bank loan or line of credit; this figure is greater than 20 percent in the Middle East and North Africa region as a whole. No firm in Erbil or Sulaymaniyah reported using banks to finance investments, but a few firms report using banks to finance working capital (6.9 percent in Erbil and 1.4 percent in Sulaymaniyah).

The microfinance sector in Iraq has grown significantly over the past 10 years, from a very low base. Two larger MFIs control more than half the market in Iraq. Thirty-eight percent of the outstanding portfolio is held by CHF, and 18 percent is held by Al Thiqa. Ten other smaller MFIs thus hold the remaining 44 percent of the outstanding portfolio. MFIs currently do not offer savings, insurance, or payments and transfer services. Before the recent escalation of violence due to ISIS and associated economic and social instability, outreach in Erbil, Sulaymaniyah, and Dohuk governorates was estimated to be approximately 15,198 loans outstanding valued at $29 million, representing 20 percent of the overall market share (based on percentage share of outstanding loans) (see Appendix I on the Iraq microfinance sector).

Trade

KRI's total imports were estimated to be about $20.8 billion. Import data provided by the KRG Ministry of Trade and Industry indicate that imports were about one-third of overall Iraqi imports and valued at about $20.8 billion in 2013. This import estimate may seem high given that KRI has only about one-tenth of Iraq's GDP and one-seventh of Iraq's population. The relatively large share of imports could, nevertheless, arise because even imports destined for other parts of Iraq come through KRI. In this case, the "import" value includes not just KRI-destined imports, but the sum of KRI imports and transit imports. At this stage, it is not possible to estimate the relative importance of the last two categories. The Ministry of Trade and Industry has not provided export data, and the most recent year for which Iraq reported export data is 2009. "Mirror data," that is, trade data from Iraq's trading partners, suggest that Iraq's merchandise exports were $88 billion in 2013. It is hard to estimate KRG's export revenue because the bulk of the exports are oil, and it is not clear how much is being sold by KRG directly and how much through Iraq's central selling mechanism, and how much total revenue is obtained.

Turkey is KRI's main trading partner. The major trade entry point for the region is Turkey, through the Ibrahim-Khalil crossing point near Zhako. Turkish exports to Iraq are estimated between $2.8 and 3.5 billion in 2007, based on official Turkish government figures. Most imported goods are consumed in the region. Followed by Turkey, KRI's largest trading partner is the Islamic Republic of Iran. The majority of goods from the Islamic Republic of Iran to KRI flow through the official customs crossing points at Bashmakh, Haji Omran, and Perwis-Khan. Iranian trucks usually go to border transloading points where they are unloaded and their cargoes are transferred to empty Iraqi trucks. Because of the long border that Iraq shares with the Islamic Republic of Iran, it is difficult to precisely estimate the value of the unofficial black market trade conducted through unofficial Iran-KRI border crossings. The U.S. Congressional Research Service estimates that the Islamic Republic of Iran's exports to Iraq increased from $1.3 billion in 2006 to $2.8 billion in 2007, of which approximately $1 billion was imported via KRI. In addition to the land border crossings with Turkey and the Islamic Republic of Iran, goods also enter KRI by air through international airports in Erbil and Sulaymaniyah.

Impact of Crises and Stabilization Assessment

A combination of factors has been adversely affecting domestic economic activity in 2014. First, and foremost, KRG's share from the federal budget of about $12 billion a year ($1 billion per month) has been withheld, mainly because of the political gridlock in Baghdad, which resulted in the failure to approve a budget for 2014. The Ministry of Finance reports that only $1.1 billion was received in 2014. Second, the arrival of Iraqi IDPs, in addition to the refugees from Syria already in KRI, have brought further pressures on KRG. Third, ISIS-related issues seem to have affected domestic economic activity and international trade and investment. As these events more or less occurred at the same time, it is not entirely possible to assess their impacts separately on the economy and the population. Both direct and indirect costs are found. In the following discussion, available data and anecdotal evidence are reviewed, and by developing a model, simulations about the impact of IDPs and refugees on fiscal balances and welfare levels are presented.

Output, Budgetary, and Welfare Impacts of IDP and Refugee Influx

In 2014, as a result of multiple crises, both revenues and expenditures registered large declines for KRG. The actual amount that has been transferred from the central government to KRG is about $1.1 billion. KRG has been able to pay wages and salaries with lags sometimes approaching three months. The execution of an investment budget was put on hold in June, and investment spending by the public sector as of June 2014 was 60 percent of its 2013 level. Total budgetary spending was down by about 60 percent in June 2014, and it is expected to stay at that level for 2014.

As a coping strategy, the Ministry of Natural Resources has been providing support to KRG and assuming wages and salaries obligations, albeit with lags. The ministry has borrowed about $1.5 billion from the domestic private sector and another $1.5 billion from international companies and suppliers by selling its future oil output. It also exported about $1.3 billion worth of oil. The ministry has been providing wages and salaries payments as well as transfers for IDPs. The ministry estimates that they directly incurred about $1 billion to provide IDPs with basic support. These expenses include diesel imports and de facto electricity subsidies as well as health and education services. The ministry has been financing some of the investment projects, and it could be expected that it will spend about $2 billion in 2014. The rapid buildup of foreign debt at this rate, from no debt to a 12 percent of GDP level, is a source of concern and has fiscal sustainability implications.

Economic growth is projected to decline by 5 percentage points in 2014. The fiscal shock has been having a contractionary impact on the economy. Even if the fraction of remaining funds might be transferred from the central government to pay the two months of outstanding public sector salaries, this will likely fall short of fully offsetting the negative impacts of a sudden drop in public expenditures on the economy. Although national accounts for KRG are not available and what is available is inconsistent, it appears that the lack of budgetary transfers (fiscal shock), as expected, had an impact on the economy. With public and private expenditure down almost 60 percent, aggregate demand continues to be dampened, and hence GDP growth is expected to be considerably less than in the previous year. The lack of consumption and total investment data makes it difficult to assess the macroeconomic impact of reduced budgetary transfers from the expenditure side, but anecdotal evidence or unofficial data are available on the production side. Using sectoral growth rates in agriculture, industry, and services, and in consultation with the Kurdistan Regional Statistics Office (KRSO), it seems that

PHOTO 1.1
Child in Arbat Camp in Sulaymaniyah Governorate

Yezidi girl, Shada, met during the mission's camp visit, September 2014. © Sibel Kulaksiz. Used with the permission of Sibel Kulaksiz; further permission required for reuse.

GDP growth in 2014 could be 2–3 percent, down from 8 percent in 2013. Private sector activities during the first half of the year and capital spending by the government, albeit lower than in 2013, and financial support by the Ministry of Natural Resources to the government seem to have provided support for growth in 2014 and lessened the impact of reduced budgetary transfers. The KRI economy has kept running on arrears. The government has sustained consumption and met immediate IDP and refugee needs with large amounts of borrowing and arrears to public sector workers and contractors. For the time being, enough buffers were on hand for this to be effective. However, the government will not be able to sustain this into 2015 without a cash infusion, and fiscal implications are seen for what has already taken place (i.e., clearing arrears, mounting liabilities in electricity sector).

The disruption of public investment projects severely affected sectors of the economy dependent on government spending. In 2014, because of the ongoing security and budget crises, the performance of governmental contracts—with a total value of ID 14.5 trillion ($12.5 billion)—was negatively affected, because no payments have been made to the contractors since early 2014. Out of this total commitment, ID 6.4 trillion has been disbursed so far. Compensation for late payments is expected to cost an additional ID 244.4 billion in the 2015 budget. The construction sector has been particularly affected, with small companies reporting bank-ruptcy. It is likely that most ongoing fixed-price civil works contracts will be further disrupted because of delayed payments coupled with more expensive oil-based products. An additional cost is caused by inflation, which covers any increase of price of labor and materials for works planned to be constructed in 2014 but delayed for implementation in 2015. When contractors submitted their bids, they were planning to carry out the work in 2014 and included prices based on that assumption. Suspension of projects for a year will lead to market prices being affected by inflation. For this, the additional cost to absorb the price increase due to inflation is estimated at ID 220 billion.

Delayed tenders of 2014 will come at a cost. Procurement of some projects with a value of ID 3.8 trillion were canceled or stopped process-ing. Those packages will be retendered again in 2015, but they are expected to absorb additional costs for a one-year delay for inflation and the additional impact of a risk factor. Additional costs of delayed tenders for 2014 are estimated at ID 670 billion.

A macroeconomic model has been developed for the purposes of this ESIA report to simulate budgetary and welfare impacts of IDPs and refugees. Direct and indirect costs are associated with IDPs and the refugee influx, and so this model provides simulations on how welfare levels among the population may evolve as a result of the crises. Return scenarios for IDPs and refugees are projected as costs depending on their duration of stay. The analysis first considers an impact analysis and later stabilization assessment that can be taken as indication of miti-gating the impact of IDPs on welfare. The findings show significant welfare-related issues and costs. The diagram of the structure of the simu-lation model for this analysis is presented in Appendix C. The modeling framework built for simulating the macroeconomic impact of IDPs and refugees is discussed in Appendix D.

Public revenues declined in 2014. These numbers are projected by considering a rule of thumb for long-term movement (using a GDP share of about 50 percent for the KRG budget). One-off deviations from this are performed to broadly match the revenue movements as indicated by the budget numbers received from the authorities. The drop in 2014 revenues is calculated by deducting the direct oil revenues, informal debt issuances, and partial transfers from Baghdad from the required transfers (shown by the counterfactual calculation; see figure 1.8).

Direct costs are high for KRG as measured by transfers to IDPs and refugees. The cost of providing IDPs with basic needs such as food, shelter, and health services is a direct fiscal impact for KRG. Under an assumption that the direct transfers (for example, those expenditures that are exclu-sively for the displaced, which do not cover other public goods and

FIGURE 1.8
Public Revenues: Baseline and Counterfactual (No Budget Shock) Scenarios, 2011–15
dollars, billions

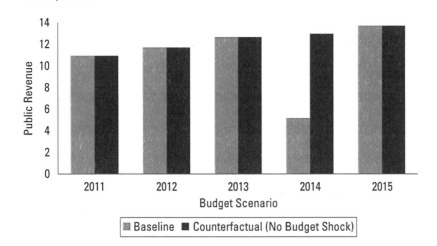

services) to IDPs and refugees have been $1,000 per person in 2014; these will stay at the same rate in 2015.

The simulated impact of the arrival of IDPs on the monetary well-being of KRI residents is projected to be about $910 million in 2014. The change in the welfare of residents driven by rapid IDP inflows is estimated by the model. To this effect, the monetary values of private consumption (GDP minus the government budget, defined in per capita terms) and access to public goods and services are assumed (produced by government, and accessed by everyone in society, including IDPs). A key assumption here is that the IDP inflow by itself does not change the aggregate private consumption of KRI residents, mainly because these goods are rival and excludable, and no externalities are seen in net terms.[3] However, IDPs also share public goods and services provided for KRI residents (e.g., roads, communications networks, and security), and it is assumed that, despite calling them public goods, these goods are nonexcludable but rival. As a result, a large number of IDPs limits the access of services for the host community. Figure 1.9 shows the simulated impact of IDP arrival on monetary well-being of KRI residents in 2014. Baseline calculations show that this amount is expected to be about $910 million in 2014.[4]

The opportunity cost of diverting budget allocations from investment spending to transfers to IDPs is high. The impact of IDPs on the monetary well-being of KRI residents has both short- and medium-term characteristics. This is true even if the IDPs stay for only one year. KRG will divert funds from investing in public capital to transfers to IDPs for at least

FIGURE 1.9
Point Impact of IDPs on Monetary Well-Being of KRI Residents, 2014
dollars, millions

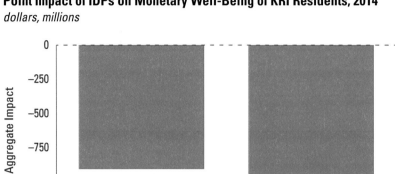

one year. As a result, the following year's public capital stock will be lower. Thus, a loss will occur in the level of public goods and services. The methodology employed in this analysis captures both the direct cost of spending for IDPs and the indirect cost (opportunity cost) on domestic residents in the form of foregone provision of public goods and services, contemporaneously.

The amount of funds required to offset the impact of IDPs on KRI residents is estimated at $1.48 billion in 2015. The following question is estimated by the model: "What is the level of funds that should be offered to KRI residents to compensate them so that, in 2015, they will have the same monetary well-being as in a case where IDPs never arrived in KRI?" The required funds depend on the extent of transfers from KRG to the IDPs and on the actual numbers of IDPs that would cohabitate the region in 2015. With current transfer schemes (about $1,000 per IDP per year) and a baseline IDP return scenario, the funds that can help stabilize the monetary well-being of KRI residents amount to about $1.48 billion in 2015.

Impact On Prices

The escalation of the conflict has resulted in price increases for rent and, to a lesser extent, for food in all three KRI governorates. Rent prices—which account for just over 20 percent of the consumer price index (CPI) basket—rose by 11.6 percent in Erbil, 12.3 percent in Dohuk, and 5.4 percent in Sulaymaniyah between January and October 2014 relative

FIGURE 1.10
Level of Consumer Price Index, January 2010 through September 2014
consumer price index, 2007 = 100

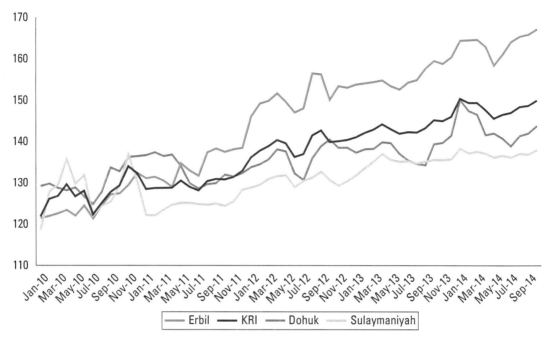

Source: KRSO.

to the corresponding period in 2013 (figure 1.10). This comes as a result of the massive influx of IDPs and refugees to the region, the lack of space, the postponement or termination of construction projects, and the lack of labor. Food prices—which account for close to 30 percent of the CPI basket—rose by 4.6 percent in Erbil between January 2014 and October 2014 relative to the same reference period in 2013 and to a lesser extent in the other two governorates. This is explained by the lack of infrastructure and resources needed to satisfy the food requirements of a larger population.

Moreover, prevailing civil insecurity and associated access problems and transport disruptions have affected the supply of fuel and transportation. Between September 2013 and September 2014, the price of fuel (gasoline, kerosene, and liquid propane gasoline) spiked to 26.5 percent in Sulaymaniyah and 25.5 percent in Dohuk. The CPI price of transportation surged to 15.2 percent in Erbil, 14.3 percent in Dohuk, and 13.8 percent in Sulaymaniyah. Electricity and water supply prices increased by 30.8 percent in Erbil and 11 percent in Sulaymaniyah.

Although the impact of the conflict has been relatively modest on prices so far, inflationary pressures on the economy are likely to be significant. The combination of the budget cut and the increasing funding requirements of Peshmerga have induced KRG to raise gasoline prices from ID 500 to ID 900 and to double the price of diesel—which is used by local generators to provide electricity to the local population during power outage—from ID 415 to ID 950. These price increases are expected to lead to a second-round effect on average prices.

Trade and Investment Impacts of IDP and Refugee Influx and ISIS

The ISIS crisis has had a significant effect on trade flows. The monthly goods trade data from Iraq's partners show a decline between May and July 2014 in Iraq's exports by about 25 percent and in its imports by 45 percent (figure 1.11). Furthermore, the ISIS crisis overlapped with the budget crisis, to which we can attribute 25–33 percent of the decline in KRG's imports (box 1.1). The budgetary crisis also induced KRG to export directly about $1.3 billion of oil beginning in May 2013.

Imports from Turkey declined significantly. The general picture of declining trade is corroborated by Turkish sources. Turkish exports to Iraq declined from $1.04 billion in May to $582 million in July 2014 (figure 1.12). Metal products, electrical equipment, foodstuffs, and plastic products are items whose exports decreased the most in absolute terms. On the other hand, exports of Iraq to Turkey—much smaller to begin with—do not seem to be affected much. Iraq exports in June and July 2014 were well above their level in 2013 and in line with export figures

FIGURE 1.11
Iraq: Trade Flows (Including Oil), January 2014 through July 2014
dollars, millions

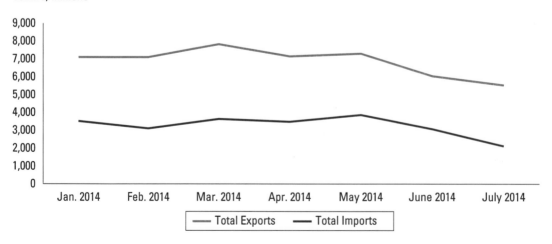

Source: Global Trade Atlas 2014.

BOX 1.1
Accounting for the Impact of the Budget Freeze

The failure to pass the 2014 budget in Iraq has led to a freeze in transfers from the national budget to KRG. The budgetary transfer from Baghdad to Erbil was normally about 12 percent of Iraq's oil revenues (17 percent of oil revenues minus KRG's contribution to the cost of the Iraqi government's sovereign functions). The monthly transfer amounted to about $1 billion. In the year 2014, transfers were received (late) for the months of January and February, but no further transfers are expected in 2014. So the net reduction in transfers is expected to be $10 billion for the year. Against this reduction in inflows, KRG conducted oil sales of about $1.3 billion and borrowed from abroad (possibly against future oil sales) about $1.5 billion (according to the Ministry of Natural Resources). The net reduction in inflows is therefore about $7.2 billion [i.e., 10 − (1.3 + 1.5)]. Recent estimates of KRI's GDP suggest a value of about $20 billion. Given the limited reliability of these estimates, it seems reasonable to assume that the reduction in national income due to the cut in transfers is in a range between one-quarter and one-third. The elasticity of expenditure on imports with respect to GDP can be assumed to be 1 (i.e., a 1 percent reduction in GDP reduces expenditure on imports by 1 percent). Therefore, we can probably attribute about one-quarter to one-third of the reduction in imports to the cut in budgetary transfers from Baghdad.

FIGURE 1.12
Iraq: Monthly Imports from Neighboring Countries, January 2014 through July 2014
dollars, millions

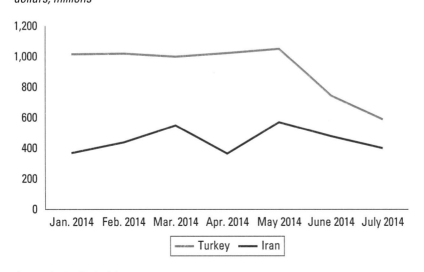

Source: Global Trade Atlas.

FIGURE 1.13
Iraq: Monthly Exports to Neighboring Countries (Including Oil), January 2014 through July 2014
dollars, millions

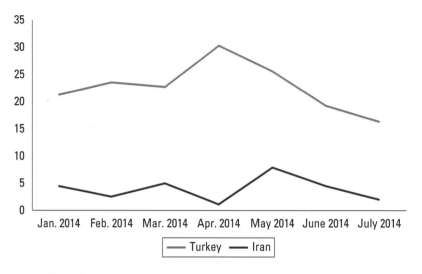

Source: Global Trade Atlas.

realized during the first five months of 2014 (figure 1.13). Further affecting the picture is the budgetary crisis that induced KRG to export directly about $1.3 billion of oil beginning in May 2014. Figure 1.14 shows sharp decline in customs revenues in June from the Ibrahim Khalil border crossing point with Turkey and Bashmakh customs with the Islamic Republic of Iran.

The Syrian IDP crisis seems to have had a relatively small direct effect on KRI's trade and investment. Three reasons can be given for this conclusion. First, Syria's share in the trade and investment of Iraq as a whole is small. On the export side, Syria accounted for only 0.6 percent of Iraq's exports in 2010 (precrisis). This small share reflects the fact that oil dominates Iraq's exports—accounting for more than 98 percent of gross annual exports in the period 2004–13—and Syria was not a major destination for oil exports. (Even for nonoil exports, Syria's share was only about 8 percent.) On the import side, Syria accounted for only one-tenth of Iraq's imports. Second, the trends for aggregate exports and imports do not show any significant adverse impact of the Syrian civil war, which began in 2011. Third, since KRI's trade is skewed toward the Islamic Republic of Iran and Turkey more than Syria, the impact of the Syrian crisis on KRI's trade is likely to have been even more limited. The share of the Islamic Republic of Iran and Turkey in KRI's imports was 51 percent in 2009 and 58 percent in 2013; these two countries' share of Iraq's imports was 36 percent in 2009 and 42 percent in 2013.

FIGURE 1.14
Customs Revenues, January 2013 through August 2014
ID, billions

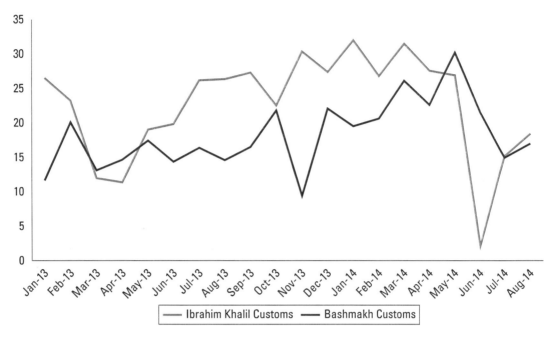

Source: KRG Customs Authorities.

Services exports have declined because of reduced transit trade and tourism. A significant part of Iraq's trade with Turkey takes place through KRI. It is reported that the number of trucks entering through the Ibrahim Khalil customs post with Turkey have declined from more than 3,000 per day to about 600 per day. To the extent that KRI transporters have a stake in the transit trade, a decline in their earnings likely occurred. Telecommunications sector is also affected. KRI-based telecommunications companies with Iraq-wide licenses and operations lost their control over an estimated 10–15 percent of their towers in Iraq and thus far have not been able to regain control over them. The ISIS crisis has also led a dramatic reduction in tourism: Tourist inflows, which had increased by 33 percent in 2013 to nearly 3 million, are reported to have declined to less than 800,000 in the first six months of 2014 (figure 1.15).

Transport and trade costs have increased because of rising fuel costs as well as changes in trade volumes. KRI's role as a transit trade route to southern Iraq has been affected. The ISIS surge diverted trade to alternate routes, mainly via the Islamic Republic of Iran, disrupting business activity in the KRI-based logistics, transport, and trading sectors (map 1.1). The diversion of trade from Turkey to Baghdad and southern Iraq via the

FIGURE 1.15
Tourist Arrivals in KRI, 2012–14
millions

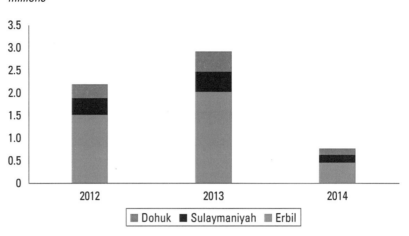

Source: KRG Ministry of Planning.
Note: The data for 2014 are for the period January to June.

MAP 1.1
Diversion of Trade Routes

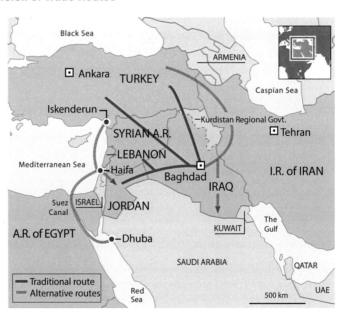

© Financial Times. Used with the permission of Financial Times; further permission required for reuse.

border crossing at Gurbulak adds more than 1,000 kilometers to the journey and costs an estimated extra $2,000 per truck, according to Turkey's International Transporters' Union. Firms operating in ISIS-affected and -controlled areas had to stop their business there. KRG was obliged by the crisis to source from refineries much farther south, leading to an increase in the price of fuel—ranging from 14 percent in Sulaymaniyah to 15 percent in Erbil and 23 percent in Dohuk—which fed through into higher electricity and transport costs. The fact that trucks carrying imports into KRI were returning empty rather than with exports from the rest of Iraq would also lead truckers to charge higher freightage for the incoming traffic. Furthermore, the crisis affected transportation to the rest of Iraq. As a result, the public distribution system delivery led to temporary reductions in availability.

Foreign direct investment flows have declined, and operations of foreign enterprises have been adversely affected. The year 2013 had seen a doubling of total investment projects to a total value of about $12.4 billion, of which more than 40 percent were foreign or joint ventures. The combination of the ISIS crisis and the budget freeze has had a chilling effect on all investment, which has declined by two-thirds so far in 2014. National investment is less than one-half and foreign investment less than one-tenth of the levels in the preceding year. Particularly striking is the decline in the share of foreign investment between 2013 and 2014 from more than 40 percent to 5 percent as a consequence of the uncertain political and economic climate. For example, Erbil Steel, which produced 18,000 tons of steel bars every month, evacuated its 600 foreign workers in June and closed its facility. Another example is the cement sector, which stopped supplying the southern market for several months. One investor has also put on hold plans to bring Starbucks to Erbil.

Welfare costs for KRI citizens as a consequence of the increase in trade costs are crudely estimated to be an annualized amount of $561 million, or $112 per citizen per year. This number can be seen as the "impact assessment" of the ISIS crisis. If the trade costs are equally distributed over citizens and the refugees and IDPs, then the aggregate compensation required (or "stabilization needs") is estimated to be $673 million per year. The stabilization interventions could take the form of offsetting actions—for example, customs reform or road improvements—which reduce trade costs. These welfare estimates do not include the even harder-to-quantify costs of the decline in services trade and foreign direct investment. The calculations and estimates of the economic impact of the ISIS crisis attributable to trade are presented in Appendix H.

Private and Financial Sector Assessment

The ISIS crisis had an impact on the private sector through five key mechanisms. First, during periods of heavy fighting, the KRI private sector faced reduced or constrained access to the southern Iraq market. For about three months (approximately June to August 2014), intense fighting against ISIS largely blocked the circulation of goods, services, and persons by road from KRI to southern Iraq. Second, KRI's role as a transit trade route to southern Iraq was severely affected. Third, firms operating and servicing in ISIS-affected or -controlled areas have reduced access to these densely populated areas. Fourth, increased insecurity inflated operating costs and decreased profitability. Fifth, the repatriation of expatriate staff and decrease in international business travel to KRI meant less business for sectors (for example, tourism and hospitality) that sell services and goods to this consumer segment. The impact of the crisis on the private sector is thus primarily felt because of increased insecurity. For example, most construction projects, being predominantly public investments, have stopped because KRG is no longer able to make installment payments because of the budget crisis.

Reduced or constrained access to the southern Iraq market has affected those industries that were largely selling to that market. KRI is seen by large firms as the secure gateway to markets in the rest of Iraq, which encompass 30 million inhabitants. Parts of the manufacturing sector in KRI, such as cement, cater to the rest of Iraq, as do KRI-based telecommunications companies. The business plans and profitability of these firms rely on being able to tap the full Iraq market. Reduced or constrained access to the southern Iraq market resulted in some firms stopping production altogether (lost sales). This was particularly true for sectors in which diversion of trade routes (via the Islamic Republic of Iran), more expensive air cargo, or premium transport prices made their sales uncompetitive—the cement business, operating on a high-volume, low-margin basis, being a case in point.

Because of increased insecurity in some parts of the country, many firms are facing increased operating costs and decreased profitability. As some trade routes were effectively blocked, some firms diverted their freight to alternative, more expensive road (via the Islamic Republic of Iran) or air routes (via Doha to reach Baghdad), or paid a hefty security premium for road transport through ISIS-controlled areas. The air freight alternative increased transportation costs a hundred-fold. Firms have put in place contingency measures, such as relying more on local procurement (rather than centralized procurement and related economies of scale), increasing warehouse facilities, and keeping larger stocks, including those for critical infrastructure that might need replacement (for example, generators for towers of mobile phone operators).

The KRI financial sector has been particularly affected by the budget crisis, which led to a shortage of cash in KRI, which in turn led to a lack of liquidity in commercial banks, with clients unable to access their deposits or to cash checks—which further eroded public trust in the banking sector. In May 2014 the general manager of the Central Bank of Iraq branch in Erbil reported that banking sector activity was down by 25 percent because of the delay in the budget transfer from Baghdad to Erbil. The delays in budget transfer also led to the nonpayment or delayed payment of civil servants—salaries, which in turn led to repayment delays for consumer loans, in particular.

The disruption of KRI public investment projects has also affected the banking sector. KRG was no longer able to pay its contractors, which in turn affected the repayment capacity of the contractors for loans from commercial banks. Banks are reporting that they are rescheduling and refinancing loans to address the impacts of the budget delays. The launch of the Erbil Stock Exchange has been postponed in view of the recent crises and their impact on the local economy.

The microfinance sector has also been affected by the budget crisis. MFIs in KRI are reporting significant repayment delays, and the crisis exacerbated their existing operational weaknesses. The result has been the deterioration of MFI operational practices, resulting in an increase in portfolios at risk and a slowdown of lending activity. Various MFIs operating in areas now controlled by ISIS had to suspend their activities.

The private sector in KRI developed immediate coping mechanisms. For the domestic and international private sector, the focus has been on maintaining operations and services, which required the development of creative (and expensive) solutions to maintain the circulation of goods and services across the country (e.g., relying on air travel via Doha to reach Baghdad, increasing inventory). Although focusing on maintaining operations, numerous actors have postponed noncritical new investments and are sitting on the fence. Strong domestic actors, especially the few large groups involved in a broad range of economic activities, have made a point of pursuing their investments in these challenging circumstances (for example, opening new hotels in Sulaymaniyah).

Notes

1. In the absence of national accounts for KRG, KRSO estimates the GDP based on estimated share in Iraq's overall GDP. According to KRSO, KRI's GDP is estimated at between 14 and 20 percent of Iraq's overall GDP. KRSO is currently working with the RAND Corporation to calculate nominal and real GDP data for KRG.

2. For Iraq as a whole, oil production was at 2.98 million barrels per day, and exports at 2.39 million barrels per day (including KRG).

3. Additional demand created by the IDPs, by itself, does not lead to an increase in the prices of imported consumption goods, which constitute a large share of private consumption. In nontraded sectors, such as housing, however, an increase in demand due to larger population could very well lead to an increase in equilibrium prices. This leads to a reduction in consumer surplus and an increase in producer surplus simultaneously; for example, renters lose but landlords gain from the rise in prices. With imperfectly elastic demand and supply schedules, the larger effect is likely to be greater. However, the difference is likely to be small, and the analysis here assumes that these two effects cancel each other. Note that the trade analysis focuses on changes in production costs triggered by changing energy costs, which affects the supply schedule. However, this effect is mainly attributed to the ISIS crisis and not to IDPs.

4. Note also that the impact would be greater had there been no budgetary shock. This is driven by two factors. First, without IDPs, more resources are allocated to provision of public goods and services. Second, without IDPs there is no congestion effect; for example, public goods are used only by the host community. In the absence of a budgetary shock, the differences in investments for public goods between IDP and no-IDP scenarios, and in what is crowded out, are greater. However, the total welfare is obviously greater in a no-budget crisis case despite this impact.

CHAPTER 2

Social Development Impact
of the Conflict

The growing inflow of Syrian refugees and internally displaced Iraqis into the Kurdistan Region of Iraq in 2012–14 has imposed substantial strains on the social sectors. This influx has put significant pressures on the public finances of the regional government and severely constrained the delivery of health, education, and social protection programs to the population. Not surprisingly, the standard of living of the population has deteriorated, and many people have fallen into poverty or are vulnerable to falling into poverty. As a result of the multiple crises, the poverty rate for KRI doubled, from 3.5 percent in 2012 to 8.1 percent in 2014.

The inflow of the displaced into KRI has led to a noticeable decline in humanitarian outcomes. The provision of basic social services in KRI has been severely affected, and the situation of those who have fled because of the conflict is dire. Despite the best efforts of the government and the international community, a significant number of refugees and IDPs lack basic necessities such as health services, education, shelter, food, and social protection. Furthermore, the influx of people has had significant potential implications for the delivery of public services given the government's limited available resources. Indeed, the crisis has reduced per capita spending in social services as a result of increased population and reallocation of resources to priority areas. Food security is hampered, and more than 243,000 IDPs are in need of shelter. The social cohesion of the population might be severely undermined should these needs fail to be addressed.

The total stabilization cost for addressing the humanitarian crisis is estimated to range between $845.9 million and $1.6 billion across the baseline and high scenarios in 2015. Within the health sector, significant spending in primary health care (PHC) and hospital services for refugees and IDPs is needed inside and outside of camps. Capital investments are also necessary to maintain adequate hospital service delivery. In the education sector, funding is needed to address the needs of the displaced and host communities. Given the distance of camps from school facilities and the fact that classrooms are already largely overcrowded, substantial capital spending will initially be needed to establish school caravans. In addition, swift action will need to be taken by the authorities to evacuate schools currently occupied by IDPs by relocating them to appropriate shelters to ensure that the host community can resume their school year. The stabilization needs for health, education, food security, poverty, and shelter are estimated to be $845.9 million for 2015. In the case of a high scenario, with an additional influx of 100,000 Syrian refugees and 500,000 Iraqi IDPs into KRI, the stabilization needs for these sectors are estimated at $1.6 billion for 2015.

Health Sector

The convergence of a massive influx of IDPs and a protracted budget crisis in 2014, in particular, have tested the ability of KRG to respond to the growing health needs of the refugee and IDP populations. Both crises have negatively impacted per capita health spending of the host community, costing approximately $46 million. The loss of these financial flows at a per capita level for the host community in KRI has potential implications for overall health system performance, including equity and responsiveness of the system. Although international partners have striven to support the KRG in managing the impact of these effects, significant financial resources are still required to restore stability to the health sector and to enable the KRI health authorities to cope with additional influx scenarios in 2015. In a low-influx scenario, the total stabilization cost for January to December 2015 adds up to a little more than $317 million, which translates to nearly $338 per refugee per IDP. It is important to note that this stabilization cost is assumed to go on top of the expected annual 2015 health sector budgets. An annotated methodology for health sector impact and stabilization calculations is presented in Appendix K.

Baseline: Health Sector Trends

Health expenditures in KRI followed a positive trend in 2008–11. The increase in expenditure had been over and above the inflation rate and the growth in population, resulting in a real increase in per capita health expenditures. As shown in figure 2.1, recurrent per capita health expenditures in this period increased by 45 percent from $76 to $110.

FIGURE 2.1
Per Capita Health Expenditures in KRI, 2008–11
dollars, inflation adjusted

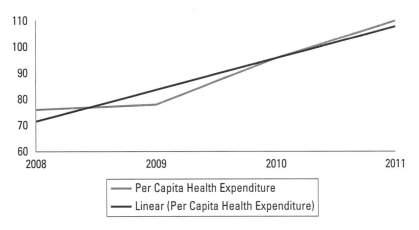

Source: Raw data on health spending and population reported by the Ministry of Health and KRSOI, respectively. Expenditure data were adjusted by inflation rate.

Public investment projects have been delivered in the health sector. Available data show that 35 new PHC facilities and nine new hospitals were built in 2008–9. In this same period, 380 new hospital beds and 25 new operation rooms were added to existing hospitals (figure 2.2).

Public spending on health relative to total government spending in KRI stands at 5.5 percent, which compares favorably to that of the national aggregate for Iraq. According to the latest National Health Accounts data for Iraq, public sector health spending out of the total public sector spending in 2008 was about 4.8 percent. In comparison, in the same year KRI recorded a 5.5 percent increase in health spending. These percentages are comparable to other middle-income countries in the Middle East and North Africa (MENA) region but lower than levels in Organisation for Economic Co-operation and Development (OECD) countries.

Health service delivery and health financing have been, and continue to be, a mix of public-private participation and investment. Public sector services are administered by the Ministry of Health in Erbil, which owns and operates a large network of primary and secondary health care facilities. These facilities are financed through general revenues and follow traditional line-item budgeting processes. The Ministry of Finance approves an annual allocation for Ministry of Health services, and all employees are salaried staff under civil service guidelines. Alongside the

FIGURE 2.2
KRG Capital Investment, 2008–11

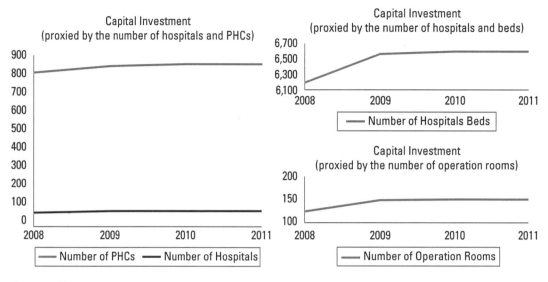

Source: KRSO.

public sector, investment in private health facilities across the region is also present. These facilities are financed largely by direct out-of-pocket payments. Figure 2.3 shows the distribution of health infrastructure by region and by public-private mix.

KRI witnessed remarkable improvements in health status as evidenced by achieved progress in infant and child mortality, immunization coverage, and under-five nutritional status, but concerted efforts are still required to maintain gains and realize further improvements. Infant mortality was estimated at 28 deaths per 1,000 live births in KRI in 2011, contrasting with the 32 deaths per 1,000 live births registered in the rest of Iraq. Similarly, child mortality averaged 32 deaths per 1,000 live births in KRI, and the general child mortality rate for the remainder of the country was estimated at 37 deaths per 1,000 live births. With respect to immunizations, about 47 percent of children under five years of age in KRI were inoculated with all recommended vaccines in 2006. This percentage increased to 64 percent by 2011. Indicators for childhood nutrition for children under age five in KRI who suffer from underweight, wasting, and stunting are 7, 5, and 15 percent, respectively. The last two indicators are comparable to figures for the rest of the country—although the prevalence of stunting in the central and southern regions of Iraq is significantly higher—about 25 percent of children under the age of five. Overall, stunting, as a measure of child nutrition, has declined faster than in the rest of Iraq (KRSO and UNICEF 2011).

FIGURE 2.3
Number of Hospital Beds, by Governorate and Public-Private Mix

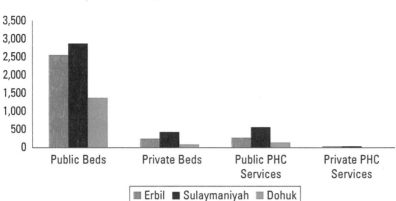

Source: KRSO 2011.
Note: PHC = primary health care.

Impact Assessment: Health Sector

Impact assessment of Syrian refugees and Iraqi IDPs for the health sector was modeled using standard adopted methodology. The impact assessment, under this methodology, is measured by estimating the difference between the actual spending for the variable of interest in period t (actual spending) and the spending that would have occurred in period t had the refugees and IDPs crises not occurred (counterfactual spending). The variable of interest used for the impact assessment in the health sector is annual health expenditure. In the absence of available and updated data on overall spending flows within the KRI health system (including government, private and donor recurrent and capital expenditures, and private out-of-pocket expenditures), data on annual recurrent expenditure by KRI's Ministry of Health are used as an alternative. Population data used come from KRSO.

Contrary to expectations, recurrent health expenditures in 2012 and 2013 did not increase in response to the Syrian refugees crisis. Once annual recurrent expenditures are adjusted by the corresponding inflation rate of that year, using KRSO's estimates of KRI's CPI for the health sector, the 2012 and 2013 expenditures fall within the spending trend of previous years (figure 2.4). Although it would have been expected that expenditures would have increased given the influx of the Syrian refugees, a series of factors undermined the KRI Ministry of Health's capacity to adjust its annual budget in response to this crisis. The first wave of Syrian refugees came as a surprise late in October 2012, with

FIGURE 2.4
Recurrent Health Expenditure in KRI, 2007–13
inflation adjusted, millions of dollars

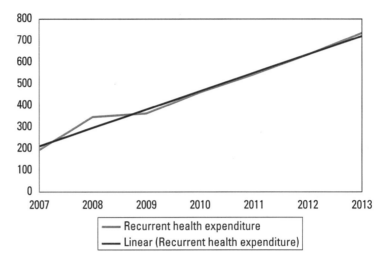

Source: Raw data reported by the KRG Ministry of Health.

six other waves adding to the refugee population throughout 2013 (Jennings 2014). The different timing of the several influx episodes, coupled with the limited available data on the fluctuating number of refugees in KRI in such a brief period, made public planning increasingly difficult at the regional level. Moreover, KRG's ability to adjust its budget would have also been contingent upon the national government's responsiveness to the crisis.

The Syrian refugee crisis negatively impacted per capita health expenditure in 2012 and 2013. From the outset of the crisis, KRG extended access to free public health services to Syrian refugees. However, with no increase in public recurrent health expenditure, per capita health spending went down as a result. This potentially could have negatively impacted overall system performance. To estimate the magnitude of the impact in per capita spending, and in the absence of utilization data,[1] the following assumptions were adopted:

PHC-hospital distribution of budget: The World Health Organization's 2011 Health Expenditure Review of the Basic Health Services in Iraq estimates that approximately 20 percent of the public recurrent health spending in Iraq flows to PHC services, and the remaining 80 percent is allocated to hospital services. This estimation is based on a sample of 162 facilities, of which 18 are located in the KRI (16 PHC facilities and two hospitals).

For the purposes of this work, it is assumed that this distribution in budget allocation is externally valid for the KRG.

PHC and hospital utilization levels for Syrian refugees: Although data on burden of disease and utilization rates for Syrian refugees are limited, anecdotal evidence suggests that the burden of disease among Syrian refugees is higher than that of the host community in KRI. Moreover, based on findings from field site visits to refugee camps in Dohuk and Sulaymaniyah, it was evident that refugees were at high risk of developing disease as a result of increased exposure to numerous environmental factors (for example, poor water and sanitation facilities), as well as increased nutrition vulnerability of women and children under five. In light of this, higher utilization levels of both PHC and hospital services would be expected. However, anecdotal evidence suggests that a large proportion of refugees forego needed health care as a result of access barriers to public health services, namely, the distance to facilities and discretionary fees charged to refugees at the facility level. The analysis differentiates between utilization rates of out-of-camp refugees and those living within camps. For out-of-camp refugees, the assessment conservatively assumes that utilization rates among refugees are similar to those of the host community, despite a higher burden of disease. As for the in-camp refugees, the analysis assumes that WHO's and UNICEF's ongoing efforts[2] to bring health services to the refugee camps have reduced refugees' health-care–seeking behaviors outside the premises of the camps. Therefore, here the assumption adopts 50 percent lower PHC and hospital utilization rates than that of the host community.

On the basis of these assumptions, PHC and hospital per capita spending were as follows (figure 2.5):

- PHC per capita spending in 2012 was reduced from a counterfactual of $25.10 to $24.89.

- Hospital per capita spending in 2012 was reduced from a counterfactual of $100.41 to $99.57.

- PHC per capita spending in 2013 was reduced from a counterfactual of $28.12 to $27.37.
- Hospital per capita spending in 2013 was reduced from a counterfactual of $112.40 to $109.46.

Such reductions amount to $21 million less in the allocation of health expenditure to the host population of the KRI in 2012–13 as a result of the Syrian refugee crisis.

In 2014 a budgetary crisis added to the ongoing Syrian refugees crisis and the recent Iraqi IDPs crisis, contributing to significantly decreasing

FIGURE 2.5
Impact on PHC Services and Hospital Per Capita Expenditures, 2011–13
dollars

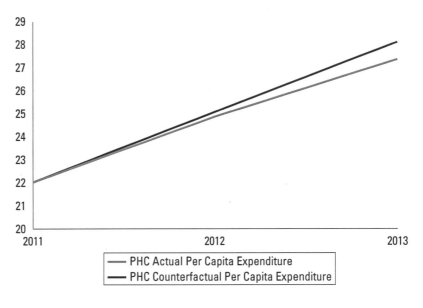

PHC Actual Per Capita Expenditure
PHC Counterfactual Per Capita Expenditure

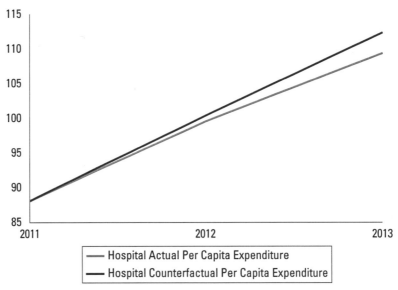

Hospital Actual Per Capita Expenditure
Hospital Counterfactual Per Capita Expenditure

Source: World Bank calculations.

the per capita health expenditure in the KRI. The overlap of these series of events has introduced a large distortionary effect on the KRG Ministry of Health's budget, making the disentangling of the fiscal impact of the Syrian refugees and Iraqi IDPs crises a complex exercise. This assessment assumes that the ministry was unable to adjust its budget to the influx of refugees and IDPs, hence attributing the entirety of the budgetary crisis to an external shock, unrelated to the refugees and IDPs crises. Against this backdrop, the ministry reported receiving a budget transfer of $179.9 million for 2014. This transfer represents only 21.1 percent of the ministry's expected 2014 recurrent budget allocation of $852.7 million and would have resulted in a proportional dramatic decrease in per capita health expenditure from $33.74 to $159.91 for this year, had the Syrian refugees and Iraqi IDP crises not occurred. Assuming the same PHC-hospital budget distribution and the levels of utilization postulated above, it is estimated that the Syrian refugees and Iraqi IDPs crises in 2014 have further plunged the per capita health expenditure of the KRI host community, from $33.74 to $29. This reduction amounts to $25.3 million less in the allocation of health expenditure to the host population of the KRI in 2014, as a result of the combined Syrian refugees and Iraqi IDPs crises that year (figure 2.6).

FIGURE 2.6

Impact of Budgetary Crisis versus Refugees and IDPs Crises on Per Capita Expenditure, 2013 and 2014

dollars

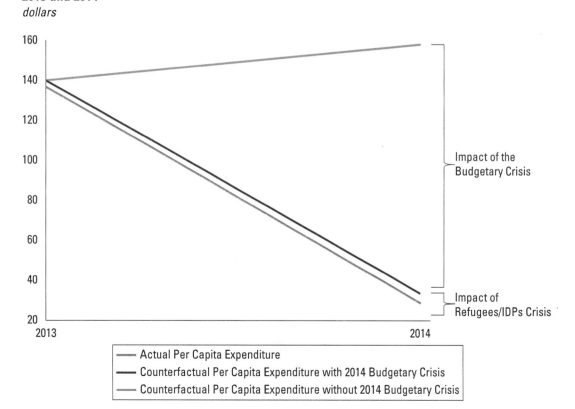

Source: World Bank calculations.

TABLE 2.1
Impact Assessment for the Health Sector, October 2012 to September 2014

Sector	Year	Counterfactual Spending ($)	Actual Spending ($)	Impact in Per Capita Spending ($)	Host Population Size	Overall Impact ($)
PHC	2012	25.10	24.89	−0.052	5,059,008	−265,897
	2013	28.12	27.37	−0.75	5,194,733	−3,936,780
	2014	6.75	5.80	−0.94	5,332,599	−5,054,841
Hospital	2012	100.41	99.57	−0.21	5,059,008	−1,063,587
	2013	112.40	109.46	−3.03	5,194,733	−15,747,122
	2014	26.99	23.20	−3.79	5,332,599	−20,219,366
Total Impact						**−46,287,596**

Source: World Bank calculations.

Overall, the difference between the counterfactual public sector per capita health spending level and the actual per capita spending affected by the refugees and IDPs influx from October 2012 to June 2014 amounts to $46.3 million. The loss of these financial flows at a per capita level for the host community in the KRI has potential implications for overall health system performance, including equity and responsiveness of the system (see table 2.1).

The calculated amount reflects the reallocation of expenditures from the host community to refugees and IDPs in 2012–14. Approximately $46 million was spent on providing health services to the refugees/IDPs community at the expense of lowering the per capita level of health expenditure of the host community.

Stabilization Assessment: Health Sector

The stabilization assessment focuses on the health spending that would be needed over the next 12 months (January to December 2015) to bring the per capita expenditure of the KRI's host community as well as the Syrian refugees and Iraqi IDPs in the region back to precrisis levels (using the 2011 level of per capita expenditure as a proxy). The assessment generates estimates for four different stabilization requirements: (1) greater health spending on recurrent and capital primary health care expenditures, and recurrent hospital expenditures engendered by greater demand from out-of-camp refugees and IDPs; (2) additional health spending on recurrent and capital PHC expenditures and recurrent hospital expenditures incurred by greater demand from in-camp refugees and IDPs; (3) necessary capital investments to maintain hospital service delivery standards; and (4) added health spending on expanded programs to maintain the public health status of the host community, Syrian refugees, and Iraqi IDPs.

The first stabilization requirement accounts for the necessary health spending on primary health care and hospital services demanded by those refugees and IDPs who reside outside the camps. The assessment assumes normative PHC and hospital utilization levels for Syrian refugees and Iraqi IDPs that are 50 percent higher than those of the host community to respond to this population's higher burden of disease. As such, it is estimated that $159.6 million is required to expand the capacity of existing PHC facilities and hospitals in KRI to accommodate the out-of-camp refugees and IDPs. On the one hand, considering the Iraqi national standard of 1 PHC facility per 5,000 population, this estimate includes PHC capital expenditures to expand infrastructure capacity in the form of 116 extensions to existing PHC centers. On the other hand, the estimate also includes the expansion of PHC staffing, medical equipment, and pharmaceuticals (for details, see Appendix K).

The second requirement focuses on providing PHC and hospital services for those refugees and IDPs residing inside organized camps. Stabilization will require the in-camp provision of PHC services and access to out-of-camp hospital services. For the latter, the assessment assumes again a normative hospital utilization level for refugees and IDPs that is 50 percent higher than that of the host community, responding to their higher burden of disease. It is estimated that $127.3 million is required to create 71 new PHC clinics (applying the Iraqi national standard of one PHC facility per 5,000 population), cover the newly built PHC facilities' recurrent costs, and expand out-of-camp hospital staffing, medical equipment, and pharmaceuticals to serve in-camp refugees' and IDPs' health needs (see Appendix K for details).

The third stabilization requirement accounts for those capital investments necessary to maintain adequate public sector hospital service delivery. Using estimates computed by the Directorates of Health in three governorates, it is estimated that approximately $4 million is required to expand the infrastructure capacity of hospitals in KRI to accommodate Syrian refugees' and Iraqi IDPs' assumed higher utilization level (50 percent more than the host community) in response to a high burden of disease. These capital investments are needed in medical equipment for public sector hospital emergency rooms and intensive care units (ICUs; see the Appendix K for details).

The last stabilization requirement revolves around the scaling up of core public health functions and the provision of psychosocial services to the refugees and IDPs. KRG needs $26.2 million to cover recommended investments in health management information systems to boost disease surveillance capacity, enhanced health communication campaigns focused on promoting hygiene and child immunizations, expanded vaccination campaigns, and rehabilitation services to respond to the mental health needs of the refugees and IDPs (see the Appendix K for details).

Stabilization figures assume that the total annual health sector budget for 2015 is allocated and maintained in accordance to KRG's 17 percent budget transfer. The total stabilization cost amounts to $317.1 million for January to December 2015, as shown in table 2.2. This figure is the amount of additional funding needed to meet the health needs of the Syrian refugees and Iraqi IDPs over the next year, while bringing the per capita expenditure of the KRI host community back to the precrisis level of 2011. It is important to note that this stabilization cost is assumed to go on top of the expected annual health sector budgets of 2015 ($995.4 million) had the budgetary crisis not occurred. The stabilization figure should also consider the amount committed by the UN and other development partners for the period in question.

Sensitivity Analyses

The model used in the stabilization assessment allows for extensive sensitivity analyses. This section provides stabilization estimates for three different influx scenarios for Syrian refugees and Iraqi IDPs in the January

TABLE 2.2
Stabilization Assessment for the Health Sector, 2015

1. Out-of-camp stabilization cost (PHC capital cost + PHC and hospital recurrent costs)	$159,551,058
2. In-camp stabilization cost (PHC capital cost + PHC and hospital recurrent costs)	127,315,774
3. Hospital capital investment stabilization cost	4,000,000
4. Programmatic stabilization cost	26,195,000
Total stabilization cost	317,061,833
Refugee/IDP per capita stabilization cost	338.21

Source: World Bank calculations.

to December 2015 period. The first influx scenario—followed so far in the previous stabilization estimations—assumes the persistence of the status quo. The second scenario assumes an inflow of an additional 30,000 refugees and 250,000 IDPs. The third, worst-case, scenario assumes the inflow of an additional 100,000 refugees and 500,000 IDPs.

The sensitivity analyses assume the capacity of building additional camps to be fixed in the January to December 2015 period, notwithstanding the influx scenario. This assessment builds on the stated capacity of the UN and its development partners to build a total of 26 camps to accommodate refugees and IDPs in this period (United Nations and KRG Ministry of Planning 2014). As such, although in the status quo scenario 44 percent of the refugees and 36.34 percent of the IDPs are assumed to be living within camps, these percentages drop to 38 percent and 27.1 percent for the medium influx scenario, and to 29 percent and 22 percent for the high influx scenario in 2015.

Total stabilization costs for each influx scenario are estimated using the same PHC–hospital budget distribution and the levels of utilization postulated. A medium influx scenario raises the stabilization cost to $417.4 million, whereas a high influx scenario increases the cost to $532.5 million. In terms of per capita stabilization, the cost stands at approximately $346 for the high influx scenario, which translates to an average monthly per capita stabilization cost of roughly $29 (table 2.3).

TABLE 2.3
Stabilization Assessment, by Scenario, 2015

	Status Quo	Medium Influx Scenario	High Influx Scenario
1. Out-of-camp stabilization cost (PHC capital cost + PHC and hospital recurrent costs)	$159,551,058	$36,397,026	$342,220,989
2. In-camp stabilization cost (PHC capital cost + PHC and hospital recurrent costs)	127,315,774	141,796,953	158,722,217
3. Hospital capital investment stabilization cost	4,000,000	5,214,750	6,575,979
4. Programmatic stabilization cost	26,195,000	34,018,907	42,960,515
Total stabilization cost	317,061,833	417,427,637	532,479,700
Refugee/IDP per capita stabilization cost	338.21	342.87	346.34
Refugee/IDP per capita stabilization cost	28.18	28.57	28.86

Source: World Bank calculations.
Note: IDP = internally displaced person; PHC = primary health care.

Education Sector

The crisis has pushed to the limits the capacity of the KRI education system, which was already short of schools and teachers and had over-crowded classrooms. It is estimated that 325,000 Syrian refugees and Iraqi IDPs are children younger than 18 years of age. Most school-aged children remain largely out of the KRI education system. Among school-aged children, 70 percent of IDPs and 48 percent of refugees are not enrolled in school. Although immediate priorities are infrastructure related[3] (e.g., school renovation, classroom expansion or construction), it is equally important that teachers are deployed and paid, textbooks are provided, language barriers are addressed, and children's security and safety are ensured. In the short run, $16.3 million per month is required to provide the basic education services to school-age children of refugees and IDPs.

Baseline: Education Sector

Before the recent instability in the region (the Syrian crisis and the ISIS surge), KRG made remarkable progress in all aspects of its education system, comparing favorably with neighboring countries. Most notably, the net enrollment improved for basic and secondary education, reaching 94.1 percent and 89.1 percent, respectively, in the academic year 2012–13. Higher education also had a rapid growth in recent years, with the number of universities increasing from three in 2003 to 18 in 2009. KRG provides nearly equal gender educational opportunities. Although boys outnumber girls in basic and secondary education—in some grades by large numbers—at the postsecondary technical education and university levels, girls are more likely to continue their education than are boys.

Since 2009, KRG has been working to bring basic and secondary education to international standards, as it introduced a new, more rigorous K–12 curriculum and made education compulsory through grade 9 instead of grade 6. The education system was also restructured, moving from the previous three levels of schools into two: basic (grades 1–9) and secondary (grades 10–12). Preparation requirements for new teachers in the basic level were upgraded to require a bachelor's degree, and new basic teacher colleges were established to train new teachers. In higher education, a teaching quality assurance system and a continuous academic development program are being established. Efforts are underway to modernize curricula and learning standards to meet labor market demand. Courses and requirements in critical thinking and debate,

TABLE 2.4
KRI Basic Education: Statistics on Students, Schools, and Teachers, 2008 and 2013

	Students		Teachers		Schools	
Governorate	2008	2013	2008	2013	2008	2013
Erbil	370,897	423,801	21,034	28,572	1,526	1,670
Dohuk	345,220	370,723	17,208	21,076	1,299	1,321
Sulaymaniyah	340,592	358,902	24,839	30,328	1,411	1,386
Total	**1,056,709**	**1,153,426**	**63,081**	**79,976**	**4,236**	**4,377**

Source: KRG Ministry of Education.

languages, computer skills, and basic science have been introduced. The basic educational capacity has expanded significantly in recent years as illustrated in table 2.4.

However, substantial gaps remain in the education sector. In basic education, school capacity shortages and lack of qualified teachers remain the two major concerns. Because of weak academic backgrounds, weak retraining programs, and lack of incentives, teachers lack key skills for effective delivery of academic content. In addition, the current rates of school rehabilitation and construction of new schools do not match population growth and the expected improvement in secondary enrollment. In higher education, the main areas of recent reforms launched by KRG include improving the quality of teaching, reforming the postgraduate education system, expanding higher education via establishment of new universities, and changing the management system of higher education institutions.

Between 2004 and 2010, enrollment increased by about 67,000 new students annually, with growth greater in the intermediate (7–9) and secondary (10–12) grades. Before the recent crisis, it was estimated that enrollment would continue to grow on average by about 90,000 new students annually, which would require building about 27,000 new classrooms and training about 5,500 additional teachers every year (RAND 2014).

Impact Assessment: Education Sector

Education is one of the key sectors being affected by the inflow of Syrian refugees and Iraqi IDPs. The number of school-age Syrian children in KRI increased from 14,400 in 2012 to 48,500 in 2013 and has now reached about 55,000. The number of school-aged children among Iraqi IDPs is estimated at 270,000. The analyses show that the large majority of these children remain out of school because of economic considerations; the language barrier; the lack of school infrastructure, teachers, and school materials; complex administrative procedures for school enrollment; and other socioeconomic reasons.

The Syrian Crisis

Assessments indicate a low registration of school-age Syrian refugee children in KRI. A recent study by UNICEF showed that approximately 90 percent of school-age Syrian refugee children in noncamp settings are not attending formal education, 76 percent of whom used to attend schools while in Syria (UNICEF 2013). Enrollment in secondary education also appears to be lower than at the primary level. Children and youth, and more specifically boys, would rather be sent to work to help meet the basic needs of their families than enroll in secondary education (United Nations, NGOs, and KRG 2012).

The proportion of Syrian refugee children attending school in the different governorates in KRI, irrespective of their age group, is low. The proportion of children between the ages of 5 and 14 enrolled in schools is 17 percent in Dohuk, 10 percent in Erbil, and 6 percent in Sulaymaniyah. School enrollment is particularly low for youth between the ages of 15 and 24 (7 percent in Dohuk, 9 percent in Erbil, and 0 percent in Sulaymaniyah) (UNICEF 2013).

The language barrier is one of the main reasons that Syrian refugee children do not enroll in school. Most of the schools in KRI teach in the Kurdish language. Although some Syrian children speak Kurdish, they are often unable to read and write in Kurdish because they have received an education in Arabic while living in Syria. As an alternative to the Kurdish teaching schools, Syrian children and their families will look for Arabic teaching schools. Those schools teaching in Arabic are, however, limited and far from the low-rent accommodation areas where Syrian refugees live.

The economic factor is another main cause for the low registration of the school-age Syrian refugee children. In the urban area, 8 percent of refugee children and youth are involved with paid labor; and 21 percent are involved with domestic tasks on a full-time basis, among which 43 percent are girls (UNICEF 2013, 18). Furthermore, some schools in KRI are unable to receive refugee students (UNICEF 2013, 11).

Other reasons for the low school enrollment of Syrian children refugees in KRI are related to disability, administrative, and psychological issues.

PHOTO 2.1
Darashakran Refugee Camp in Erbil Governorate

Darashakran refugee camp profile in Erbil governorate. © UNHCR/T. Tool. Used with the permission of UNHCR/T. Tool; further permission required for reuse.

Children with disabilities are neglected in some schools. The proportion of Syrian refugee children with disabilities attending schools in KRI is 15 percent (6 percent of Syrian refugee children have some form of disability) (UNICEF 2013, 11, 18). Another impediment to children enrolling in schools, even if they wish to do so, is that they do not possess the prerequisites in terms of documentation, identification papers, or certificates. Many children do not find it easy to enroll back in school after they dropped out while in Syria. Other children are still very much affected psychologically by the experiences they went through.

Within its existing limited budget space, KRG has been supporting the educational needs of the Syrian refugees. For example, a second shift has been allocated to the Syrian refugees in some schools with the associated costs, including teacher salaries, being provided by the Ministry of Finance. KRG has also built two schools for the refugees, although they have not yet opened because no funds are available to cover teacher salaries and to pay for textbooks and school supplies.

Iraqi IDPs

The ISIS crisis in 2014 created a large inflow of Iraqi IDPs into KRI, with an estimated 270,000 school-age children among them. The crisis violently erupted during the school year in January and February 2014 in the regions affected by the crisis, and children from those areas were out of school till late 2014. The massive influx of IDPs into KRI created a humanitarian crisis and pushed to the limits the capacity of the regional government, the UN, and other donors to respond to the basic needs of the IDPs. As a result, at the peak of the crisis in October 2014, more than 450 schools across the region were used for this purpose. Some 435 of these schools were located in Dohuk, and, on the basis of data obtained earlier in the year, they were largely concentrated in the districts of Zakho, Semel, and Dohuk (table 2.5).

As experienced by the Syrian refugees, the IDP families also face a number of similar challenges in accessing the public education system, including the language barriers, associated economic costs, administrative procedures, insecurities and uncertainties associated with possible further displacements, children's safety, and other issues. KRG authorities are aware of these challenges and are taking steps to address them. For example, to address the language barrier, Arabic-speaking teachers and school instructors are being identified and trained, including those among the IDPs, and discussions are underway for school textbooks in Arabic to be supplied from the federal education ministry in Baghdad.

TABLE 2.5
Dohuk: Number of Refugee Shelters in Schools as of September 1, 2014

District	Schools with Refugees	Operating Schools	Number of Schools Occupied by Refugees
Zakho	136	0	136
Semel	110	7	103
Dohuk	164	0	164
Amede	39	33	6
Shekhan	46	39	7
Akre	94	39	55
Bardarash	64	10	54
Total	**653**	**128**	**525**

Source: KRG authorities.

Stabilization Assessment: Education Sector

Education is one of the priority areas in providing for IDPs' most immediate needs because education is a key factor in addressing the trauma experienced by the IDP children (United Nations and KRG Ministry of Planning 2014a). Priorities in this area are focused on school infrastructure, including (1) renovation and rehabilitation of schools following IDPs' relocation to proper shelters; (2) expanding classroom capacity, largely via prefabricated mobile classrooms (caravans), in existing host community schools and in camps; and (3) exploring the potential offered by underused schools in rural areas and by opening schools in urban areas. Other priority actions include (1) raising awareness and sharing information among the IDPs about the education system and the availability of spaces for IDP children and (2) procuring supplies for schools, children, and teachers.

The most immediate education sector needs are now focused on infrastructure, such as school and classroom renovation and expansion and construction of temporary classrooms and learning spaces within camps. In parallel, KRG authorities, together with the donor community, are desperately trying to find other options to host refugees and IDPs so that the schools used as shelters can be quickly rehabilitated to allow the academic year in the KRI to start at full operational status.

The KRG Ministry of Education, with the support of the donor Education Cluster, has developed an action plan that includes recommendations for the short to medium term to make sure that, beyond immediate school infrastructure needs, all necessary conditions are provided to have qualified teachers deployed and paid, textbooks and other school materials provided, language barriers addressed by identifying Arabic-speaking school teachers among Syrian refugees and IDPs, psychological and health services provided, and security and safety of children ensured.

An urgent need exists to provide additional funds to the KRG education sector to cope with the impact of Syrian refugees and IDPs. Basic and secondary education in KRI is free, and it is entirely funded by the government. However, the current level of education spending in KRI is rather modest, and is largely spent on teacher salaries, textbooks, and school equipment (table 2.6). With the precrisis delays in paying teacher salaries and procuring school supplies, KRG is not in a position to bear alone the financial costs of the Syrian refugee and IDP influx, including those for the education sector.

Roughly $16.3 million per month is required to provide basic education services to Syrian refugees and Iraqi IDPs. Stabilization costs for 2015 are estimated at $196 million under the baseline population scenario. This would include funds necessary for renovating and rehabilitation of schools currently used as shelters for the IDPs, constructing interim learning facilities via prefabricated classrooms, paying teacher salaries, and acquiring textbooks and other school supplies and equipment. This assessment is based on the assumption of a 100 percent student enrolment rate. The stabilization assessment for the education sector is presented in table 2.7.

TABLE 2.6
KRG Education Sector Expenditures, Actual Spending 2008–12
dollars, millions

	2008	2009	2010	2011	2012
Total education expenditure	1,026.3	1,052.4	1,207.1	1,407.2	1,628.3
Current expenditure	928.9	966.1	1,111.1	1,315.8	1,523.2
(% share)	90.5	91.8	92.0	93.5	93.5
Capital expenditure	97.4	86.3	96.0	91.4	105.1
(% share)	9.5	8.2	8.0	6.5	6.5

Source: KRG Ministry of Education.

TABLE 2.7
Education Sector Stabilization Assessment, 2015 Projection
dollars, millions

	Baseline Scenario[a]		Low Scenario[b]		High Scenario[c]	
	Syrian Refugees	**IDPs**	**Syrian Refugees**	**IDPs**	**Syrian Refugees**	**IDPs**
Current spending	10.5	49.9	12.3	58.5	16.6	93.0
Teacher salaries	3.0	14.3	3.5	16.8	4.7	26.6
Books and school materials	7.5	35.6	8.8	41.8	11.8	66.4
Capital spending	23.5	111.6	27.4	130.1	36.5	204.1
School rehabilitation and additional caravans	23.5	111.6	27.4	130.1	36.5	204.1

Source: World Bank calculations.
Note: IDPs = internally displaced persons.
a. Status quo—the current population of Syrian refugees and IDPs remains unchanged.
b. Additional influx of 30,000 Syrian refugees and 250,000 Iraqi IDPs.
c. Additional influx of 100,000 Syrian refugees and 500,000 Iraqi IDPs.

Food Security and Agricultural Livelihoods

Food security for KRI is hampered by disruption of transportation routes. The governorates most affected by the ISIS crisis, Nineveh and Salahaddin, on average contribute nearly a third of Iraq's wheat production and about 38 percent of its barley. Many grain silos, some of which serve KRI populations, have been captured by insurgents. Increased food demand in KRI due to increased population is being met fully by food imports. Domestic agriculture, already in decline, has been further disrupted by decreased government contracts. The cost of the public distribution system, agricultural budget support to farmers, public sector salaries, as well as food assistance to refugees and IDPs continue to dominate government expenditures.

Stabilization cost is estimated at $155 million for 2015. This estimates the funds necessary to provide basic food needs to targeted Syrian and IDP populations. Thus, this does not include cost of support for KRI families who may fall into food insecurity. It also excludes potential costs of restoring agricultural production and food logistics infrastructure that may be damaged by the fighting. This stabilization assumes that PDS and agricultural support budgets for KRG are held at precrisis levels.

Food Security and Agriculture Precrisis (Baseline) Conditions

KRI's share of Iraq's agricultural production is high. It produces 50 percent of the nation's wheat, 40 percent of its barley, 98 percent of its tobacco, 30 percent of its cotton, and 50 percent of its fruit. Its main strategic crops are cereals (e.g., wheat, barley, corn, sunflowers, and rice), vegetables (e.g., tomatoes, cucumbers, and eggplants), and fruits (e.g., grapes, apples, figs, and pomegranates). The most important export market for KRI's agricultural production is the rest of Iraq.

However, KRI's agricultural productivity has been hampered by insufficient investment as well as policy distortions. The share of government budget dedicated to agriculture is 2 percent. This is low compared with food-importing states' agricultural budgets that average 5 percent. The UN recommends 10 percent as an optimal level of investment. The agricultural budget has been misdirected to inefficient and ineffective spending, mostly for wages and subsidies, as well as price and production controls that sustain artificially low prices but also reduce agricultural producers' incentives. Public investment in agriculture is not resulting in increased yields. Crop yields in Iraq today are low by any international comparison (FAO 2012), due, in part, to the effects of prolonged wars, civil strife, sanctions, droughts, and deteriorated infrastructure for input production and research and extension services. Scope is seen to improve the effectiveness of public expenditures in agriculture.

KRI has been heavily dependent on imported food and subsidies. The primary mechanism for supporting food security is the Iraqi government's PDS and subsidies to producers. PDS, the main source of food for the poorest Iraqis, has yet to be targeted. It provides all but a few Iraqi households with subsidized basic food items. Because of the impact of PDS in large part, farmer incentives are dampened. Similarly, agricultural production as a whole is heavily subsidized, with current figures for KRG exceeding $250 million. These funds cover crop production ($200 million or 80 percent of all funds), transportation ($20 million or 8 percent of all funds), and material acquisition such as seeds, fertilizers, pesticides, and other items utilized in the growth process ($30 million or 12 percent of all funds). The largest of these subsidies relates to wheat production. For 2011, wheat was subsidized at $300 per ton, with a production target of 500,000 tons; thus, KRG spent approximately $150 million to subsidize local wheat production.

KRI households' food security and daily calorie intake levels are better than those of the rest of Iraq. Food deprivation per capita, defined by Food and Agriculture Organization methodology as the number of people whose daily dietary energy intake is lower than the average minimum dietary energy requirement for Iraq of 1,730 kilocalories per person per day, has traditionally registered at 1 percent in KRI versus 7 percent for all of Iraq. The level of per capita, per day caloric consumption in the three governorates of KRI has been much higher than that in the remainder of Iraq, with 3,100 kilocalories per person per day on average in KRI compared with 2,510 kilocalories per person per day in the central and southern governorates of Iraq. Average consumption level is highest in Sulaymaniyah Governorate with 3,300 kilocalories per person per day, compared with 2,940 in Erbil and 2,910 in Dohuk.

Impact Assessment

The impact assessment of the conflict in terms of food security is estimated at $29.8 million. This represents only the dilution of the agricultural subsidy budget in terms of indirect income transfers to KRI host communities between 2012 and 2014. The impact assessment includes an assumption that no dilution has taken place in direct income transfer to KRI host families, because transfers are direct from the government budget to registered KRI families.

Although food security in KRI has been sustained during the Syrian refugee influx, the recent IDP surge is resulting in food insecurity. Throughout the Syrian refugee influx, Syrians and the host community have remained food secure. However, during the recent ISIS crisis normal supply routes have been interrupted by insecurity, which has limited the movement of wheat and other produce in and out of KRI to Baghdad. Grain stored in government of Iraq silos in central Iraq is now being used and sold by ISIS. The ISIS offensive coincided with the wheat and barley harvests and, crucially, the delivery of crops to government silos and private traders. ISIS now controls all nine silos in Nineveh Province, along with seven other silos in other provinces. Since overrunning Mosul, ISIS has seized hundreds of thousands of tons of wheat from abandoned fields. The crisis is now threatening winter planting in Ninewa and Salah al-Din, which contribute nearly a third of Iraq's wheat.

Food insecurity is prevalent with host communities as well. Host locations are beginning to experience food shortages and price increases, the latter especially in rice. The PDS for subsidizing food staples, although operational, is not functioning optimally. Thus host communities, especially vulnerable groups within them, are also being directly impacted. PDS relies on food import routes from Turkey and Syria, as well as storage silos for distribution. Most IDPs who had access to food distribution in their home governorates no longer have access to their PDS away from their established place of residence. More than 4 million individuals in Iraq rely on the PDS for more than 50 percent of their energy intake, and approximately 1.5 million individuals in Iraq, in the lowest 20 percent income group, have already become highly food insecure and are now in need of emergency food assistance. As more and more IDPs fall into food insecurity, PDS will no longer be a resource to meet basic food needs.

Inability to distribute government-subsidized agricultural inputs will affect Iraqi farmers. In addition to the anticipated reduced harvest, farmers will likely face reduced availability of government-subsidized farming inputs—such as seeds, fertilizers, and pesticides—which affect their capacity to plant cereals for the winter 2015 season. Moreover, livestock health and productivity are severely threatened by reduced access to animal feed sources (including supplementary feeding with cereals) and veterinary supplies and services, which are likely to come to a halt in severely affected areas. As losses to production and assets increase, it will become progressively more difficult for farmers and herders to sustain or restart their livelihoods. The resulting loss of income and immediate food sources (such as eggs, milk, and fresh vegetables) over an extended period will translate into greater reliance on food assistance for KRI farmers.

Transition from distributed food to cash-and-voucher systems will test food supply and prices on the open market. Food-based humanitarian assistance to date has been in the form of meal replacement bars to transiting IDPs, food kitchens in IDP camps, and food rations (for example, rice, lentils, wheat flour, oil, and canned vegetables) to IDP families with access to cooking facilities. However, cash-and-voucher programs, to replace rations and food kitchens, are quickly being phased in. Although the voucher system affords IDPs greater flexibility than direct food distribution, this also further strains KRI commercial markets.

Distributed food to IDPs often benefits the population disproportionally. Distribution sites for recently arrived IDPs often operate first-come, first served, which disadvantages those in certain gender, age, and/or disability groups. School feedings for refugee children are being discontinued because of the depletion of external funding.

Food insecurity coping strategies are becoming apparent. The most commonly applied coping strategy to deal with the lack of food is to rely on lower quality, less expensive food, especially in more rural refugee and IDP settings. It should be noted that the coping strategy of purchasing lower quality food reinforces demand for, and supply of, low-quality, unregulated foodstuffs.

A much higher percentage of IDPs are farmers than is the current KRI population. Agriculturally employed IDPs are abandoning productive fields, as well as agricultural investments, thus guaranteeing large losses in IDP income. These same IDPs have a primary labor skill set in agriculture and may not be easily absorbed into alternative labor settings. Support is needed to restore local livelihoods and create relevant income opportunities for these rural IDPs.

Last, IDPs who flee their homes to KRI now are less likely to have host family support than those already in the region. The latest data indicate that IDPs who fled their homes in earlier stages of the conflict had family contacts inside KRI, whereas the newly displaced are less likely to have a support network in the region. Approximately 21 percent recently interviewed IDPs reportedly lack any form of support, and 77 percent planned to use personal savings. This lack of familial safety net results in a more immediate food insecurity for current and future IDPs than has been the case to date.

Stabilization Assessment

Stabilization cost for 2015 is estimated at $34 million for Syrian refugees and $121 million for Iraqi IDPs to ensure food security in KRI. Stabilization needs for baseline, low, and high scenarios are presented in table 2.8.[4] Iraqi IDPs' food needs are estimated at $31 per person per month.[5] This figure assumes a $21 per person per month baseline as the price of the food basket.[6] An increment of $10 per person per month accounts for the implicit costs of food importation, within-country transportation, storage, delivery, and/or distribution. Whether food needs are met by food rations or by vouchers, these implicit expenditures are expected to accrue and to be passed on to either the consumer or an intermediate party. It is assumed that 55 percent of Iraqi IDPs defined as "in need" will be targeted

TABLE 2.8
Stabilization Assessment for Food Security and Agricultural Livelihoods, 2015
dollars, millions

	Baseline[a]	Low Scenario[b]	High Scenario[c]
Total stabilization assessment	155.4	201.4	254.1
Syrian refugees	34.3	39.4	51.1
Iraqi IDPs	121.1	162.0	203.0

Note: IDPs = internally displaced persons.
a. Status quo—the current population of Syrian refugees and IDPs remains unchanged.
b. Additional influx of 30,000 Syrian refugees and 250,000 Iraqi IDPs.
c. Additional influx of 100,000 Syrian refugees and 500,000 Iraqi IDPs.

for food assistance.[7] This group has been defined as "those in need of life-saving, time-critical humanitarian assistance" by the UN Country Team in Iraq and is applied in all UN response plans. Syrian refugee food needs are similarly estimated at $31 per person per month, based on the same assumption as those above applied to IDP food needs. It is assumed that all Syrian refugees will be in need of food assistance to this extent, because the savings of Syrian refugees currently in KRI have been rapidly depleted, and the Syrians expected to enter will have less means than those already in the region. It should be emphasized that these estimates do not include increased food provisions for those KRI families who may fall into food insecurity because of increased competition for, and thus prices of, food.

A decreased Iraqi 2014 harvest and planting for 2015 will result in less locally available foodstuffs. The crisis affected the May–June 2014 cereal harvest and postharvest activities in key production areas, particularly within Ninewa Governorate. Although the level of damage is yet to be determined, a reduced harvest—and thus reduced replenishment of central cereal silos—are anticipated. This may cause food supply levels to drop quickly and sharply, increase import requirements, and cause food price increases. The crisis has rapidly transformed Iraq's food security prospects. Before the escalation of conflict, an above-average wheat harvest was forecast because of favorable weather conditions. Also, import requirements stood at average levels and food prices remained stable (mainly because of subsidies).

Recommencement of food distribution through the PDS throughout the country will considerably address immediate food security gaps but is detrimental to long-term national food security. This is especially true for IDPs who had access to PDS in their home governorates, but for whom PDS transfers may not be made to KRI for their access. However, in the longer term PDS undermines the domestic agricultural sector by contributing to the region's reliance on imported produce and goods.

The agricultural budget should be reoriented toward productive investment. KRG's agricultural support should shift away from subsidies toward improving access to credit, rehauling agricultural support services, expanding land plots for agricultural lease, and strengthening food safety and marketing regulations and enforcement. Medium-term support to land-leasing programs as well as small-scale agricultural and livestock support for Syrian and IDP farmers will create income opportunities.

Efforts should also focus on building and enforcing a food quality and safety regulatory structure. Lack of such to date has made KRI vulnerable for imported goods and products of an often substandard, outdated, tainted, and/or diluted nature. Food safety and quality regulations and enforcement, including endorsement of international organic certification regulations, are critical for the region.

Poverty and Welfare

The crises in Syria and Iraq have had a profound effect on the welfare of people in KRI. The most important consequence has been in terms of the massive influx of Syrian refugees and Iraqi IDPs—large in absolute terms but also relative to the population of KRI. Another important mechanism through which their welfare may have been affected is through changes in the flows of public transfers, primarily the public distribution system, and in terms of arrears in the payment of public sector salaries. The main channels of welfare impact therefore are expected to be through population changes, earnings, and transfers from government.[8] On the basis of the data available, and conservative (lower-bound) estimates for the supply of PDS goods and payment of public sector salaries, the twin crises would imply a sharp increase in poverty head-count rates in KRI of 4.4 percentage points in 2014. For 2015, based on lower and upper bound scenarios considered, between 8 and 10 percent of the persons living in the KRI are estimated to be living below the poverty line. A rough estimate of the amount of resources necessary on average to bring poverty rates down to the "without-crisis" level is estimated to range from $66.5 million to $107.8 million for 2015.

Poverty Baseline for KRG

Between 2007 and 2012, KRI added almost 1 million people (according to survey-based poverty estimates), an increase of 23 percent relative to 2007, which was a much larger increase in population relative to the rest of Iraq. For instance, the increase in population in the 15 other governorates in Iraq was about 3.2 million, or, 0.2 million on average per governorate. In contrast, on average, the Kurdistan governorates added 0.3 million persons during the same five-year period. Other evidence from the 2012 Iraq Household Socioeconomic Survey (IHSES) suggests that a significant part of the net population addition in KRI was because of the return migration of previously displaced Kurdish families.

During the same period, poverty head-count rates in KRI fell from 4.3 percent to 3.5 percent (based on a national poverty line of ID 105,500.4 per person per month in 2012). Among the three governorates in KRI, poverty rates remained almost unchanged in Erbil and Sulaymaniyah, and in Dohuk, head-count rates fell from 8.8 percent to 5.8 percent. Although KRI experienced only modest reductions in poverty, along almost all nonincome dimensions of welfare, significant improvements were seen between 2007 and 2012. Improvements in welfare as measured by per capita consumption expenditure were relatively even across the distribution, implying that although poverty did not fall much, no increase in inequality occurred.

In KRI, the low rates of consumption poverty were accompanied by low rates of poverty in human development. Compared with the rest of Iraq, KRI has the best performance in terms of nutritional measures, with stunting rates for children up to age 5 at 17 percent. The Sulaymaniyah Governorate displays the lowest rates of stunting and underweight children and the second lowest in terms of stunting in the country.

Public service delivery was better in KRI before the crisis compared with the rest of Iraq. Basic health and education services were relatively accessible for households: On average, public hospitals in KRI were 19 minutes away, relative to the national average of 23 minutes. Both elementary and high schools were accessible, within 6 and 10 minutes, respectively. In contrast to many parts of Iraq, more than 90 percent of households reported receiving electricity more than 12 hours in 2012. Access to piped water through the public grid was above 90 percent in 2012, but the percentage of households experiencing interruptions in public water supply more than once a week has increased to more than 70 percent.

KRI has made rapid advances in the education sector between 2007 and 2012. In 2007, for instance, working-age adults were relatively less educated—the share of KRI working-age adults with less than a primary education was 23 percentage points higher than the national average of 34 percent. Older generations in the region started out with much higher levels of illiteracy and incomplete primary education relative to Iraq and lower levels of complete primary education and higher education. However, outcomes have been improving over time. Gross enrollment rates in 2012 were above 100 percent even at the intermediate and secondary levels, the highest in the country. Moreover, net enrollment rates for postprimary education have increased substantially in KRI, from 48 to 61 percent at the intermediate level, and from 23 to 38 percent at the secondary level, between 2007 and 2012.

Labor market outcomes have also improved in KRI during 2007–12, and the region witnessed an economic revival. Male labor force participation increased between 2007 and 2012 to reach the national average of 70 percent and was accompanied by an increase in male employment rates and a relative shift toward full-time work. The bulk of this increased employment for men in the region was concentrated in the financial, insurance, and professional services sector, which accounted for one-fifth of all male employment in 2012. However, male underemployment remains widespread.

In KRI 42 percent of total income derives from nonlabor income and transfers. Dependence on PDS rations accounts for 20 percent of nonlabor income on average. However, it is higher for the bottom decile: In KRI, PDS rations account for 42 percent of nonlabor income for the bottom decile. It is plausible that the abnormal increase in the KRI population muted welfare improvements.

Macroeconomic Projections: Transmission Channels for the Welfare Impact of Shocks

A microsimulation model is used to evaluate the welfare and distributional impacts of the Syrian refugee and IDP influx in the three governorates of KRI. This microsimulation model,[9] which can be implemented through ADePT, is flexible in that it can account for multiple transmission mechanisms and capture impacts at the microlevel across the income distribution. In particular, the model can take into account large changes in population, labor market adjustments in employment and earnings, nonlabor incomes including public transfers and remittances, and price changes (including variations in food and nonfood prices). The macroeconomic variables used as inputs into the microsimulation are intended to capture most of the transmission channels and are the following: (a) large changes in population, (b) changes in growth and employment, (c) changes in earnings, in particular, public sector salaries and public transfers, and (d) price changes. The methodology is discussed in Appendix J.

Population Growth

Demographic changes affect the welfare impact. This report defines two types of population shocks: the Syrian refugees and the Iraqi IDPs. Thus, the results are presented for each population shock separately and the total when considering both. It is important to notice the "without shock scenario" or "reference scenario" corresponds to the natural KRI population growth. Given Iraq's lack of a population census, this report estimates the natural KRI population growth as the annual population growth rate by age brackets and gender based on IHSES 2007 and 2012. The Syrian refugees' and the IDPs' population growth scenarios are based on information provided by UNHCR and Shelter Cluster and CCCM Cluster Rapid Assessment. Both sources give not only estimates of total population, but most importantly its distribution by gender and age brackets (table 2.9).

This population effect creates major problems for the labor market, in particular, and the economy as a whole to absorb them without adversely impacting their labor and welfare status. Even though the information

TABLE 2.9
Distribution of Population, by Gender and Age Range, 2014
percent

Age (years)	Syrian Refugees		Internally Displaced Persons	
	Male	**Female**	**Male**	**Female**
0–4	7.7	7.5	9.1	10.0
5–11	8.0	7.6	8.2	9.1
12–17	6.3	4.4	11.8	13.6
18–59	35.0	21.7	18.2	18.2
60+	0.9	1.0	0.9	0.9
Total	**58**	**42**	**48**	**52**

Sources: ShelterCluster and CCCM Cluster Rapid Assessment, September 10, 2014 (with REACH) and UNHCR Registration Trends for Syrian Refugees.

above is enough for estimating different scenarios, the simulation tool does not allow dividing groups into asymmetric age brackets. To tackle this difficulty, it is assumed that the distribution of the population between 18 and 59 years old is similar to that obtained for the natural growth rate, and four age brackets by gender are built. Table 2.10 presents the projection results for 2014 under the natural population growth rate assumption. However, the total population would increase by up to 30 percent in only two years as a consequence of natural growth among IDP and Syrian refugees. In addition, most of the additional population is mainly concentrated within the active population age range (18–60 years old).

No official predictions are available on how the refugee and IDP populations will evolve in 2015. The information for the Syrian refugees and IDPs population is available only for 2014. Therefore, three different scenarios are proposed for 2015: baseline, lower bound, and upper bound. In each scenario, the total population predicted will be the result of adding to the total population predicted for 2015 based on the natural population growth and different IDPs' and Syrian refugees' projections. The baseline does not consider an increase in the 2014 IDPs and Syrian refugees populations (table 2.11). In other words, the total number of IDPs and Syrian refugees remains constant as in 2014.

Low and high scenarios are taken into consideration. The lower bound includes an additional 250,000 for IDPs and 30,000 for Syrian refugees (table 2.12). The upper bound accounts for a significant increase for both IDPs and refugees populations, an additional 500,000 and 100,000, respectively (table 2.13).

TABLE 2.10
Population Projections for 2014, Different Scenarios
thousands

Age (years)	2012		2014*		2014**		2014***		2014	
			Natural Population Growth		Natural Population Growth + IDPs		Natural Population Growth + Syrian Refugees		Natural Population Growth + IDPs + Syrian Refugees	
	Male	Female	Male	Female	Male	Female	Male	Female	Male	Female
0–20	1,128.5	1,075.7	1,192.6	1,131.7	1,304.3	1,271.0	1,125.9	1,059.4	1,349.8	1,311.4
20–40	764.3	759.5	848.6	820.6	1,020.6	983.8	974.3	922.1	1,070.1	1,012.9
40–60	332.8	380.7	391.6	444.4	471.0	532.8	449.6	499.4	493.8	548.6
60+	138.2	153.1	158.4	169.8	165.4	176.8	160.2	172.0	167.2	179.0
Subtotal	2,363.9	2,369.0	2,591.2	2,566.5	2,961.3	2,964.5	2,710.1	2,652.9	3,081.0	3,051.8
Total	**4,732.9**		**5,157.7**		**5,925.8**		**5,363.0**		**6,132.8**	

Sources: *ESIA team elaboration based on IHSES 2007 and 2012; **ShelterCluster and CCCM Cluster Rapid Assessment, September 10, 2014 (with REACH); ***UNHCR Registration Trends for Syrian Refugees.
Note: IDPs = internally displaced persons.

TABLE 2.11
Population Projections, Baseline Scenario, 2015
thousands

Age (years)	2012		2015*		2015**		2015***		2015	
			Natural Population Growth		Natural Population Growth + IDPs		Natural Population Growth + Syrian Refugees		Natural Population Growth + IDPs + Syrian Refugees	
	Male	Female	Male	Female	Male	Female	Male	Female	Male	Female
0–20	1,128.5	1,075.7	1,226.0	1,160.8	1,336.2	1,295.8	1,157.8	1,084.2	1,381.7	1,336.1
20–40	764.3	759.5	894.1	853.1	1,065.1	1,016.2	1,019.2	955.4	1,114.1	1,044.9
40–60	332.8	380.7	424.8	480.2	506.0	572.0	484.2	537.8	529.3	588.2
60+	138.2	153.1	169.6	178.8	176.6	185.8	171.4	181.0	178.4	188.0
Subtotal	2,364.9	2,369.0	2,714.5	2,672.8	3,083.8	3,069.8	2,832.6	2,758.3	3,203.5	3,157.2
Total	**4,732.9**		**5,387.3**		**6,153.7**		**5,590.9**		**6,360.7**	

Sources: *ESIA team elaboration based on IHSES 2007 and 2012; **ShelterCluster and CCCM Cluster Rapid Assessment, September 10, 2014 (with REACH); ***UNHCR Registration Trends for Syrian Refugees.
Note: IDPs = internally displaced persons.

TABLE 2.12
Population Projections, Lower Scenario, 2015
thousands

Age (years)	2012		2015* Natural Population Growth		2015** Natural Population Growth + IDPs		2015 *** Natural Population Growth + Syrian Refugees		2015 Natural Population Growth + IDPs + Syrian Refugees	
	Male	Female	Male	Female	Male	Female	Male	Female	Male	Female
0–20	1,128.5	1,075.7	1,226.0	1,160.8	1,408.9	1,377.6	1,164.4	1,090.1	1,461.0	1,423.8
20–40	764.3	759.5	894.1	853.1	1,095.9	1,045.3	1,026.3	959.5	1,152.0	1,078.2
40–60	332.8	380.7	424.8	480.2	520.6	588.4	487.6	540.1	547.3	606.9
60+	138.2	153.1	169.6	178.8	178.9	188.1	171.6	181.3	180.9	190.5
Subtotal	2,364.9	2,369.0	2,714.5	2,672.8	3,204.3	3,199.1	2,850.0	2,771.0	3,341.0	3,300.0
Total	**4,732.9**		**5,387.3**		**6,403.7**		**5,620.9**		**6,641**	

Sources: *ESIA team elaboration based on IHSES 2007 and 2012; **ShelterCluster and CCCM Cluster Rapid Assessment, September 10, 2014 (with REACH); ***UNHCR Registration Trends for Syrian Refugees.
Note: IDPs = internally displaced persons.

TABLE 2.13
Population Projections, Upper Scenario, 2015
thousands

Age (years)	2012		2015* Natural Population Growth		2015** Natural Population Growth + IDPs		2015*** Natural Population Growth + Syrian Refugees		2015 Natural Population Growth + IDPs + Syrian Refugees	
	Male	Female	Male	Female	Male	Female	Male	Female	Male	Female
0–20	1,128.5	1,075.7	1,226.0	1,160.8	1,481.6	1,459.4	1,179.8	1,103.7	1,549.2	1,519.3
20–40	764.3	759.5	894.1	853.1	1,126.7	1,074.4	1,042.9	969.2	1,199.4	1,116.9
40–60	332.8	380.7	424.8	480.2	535.3	604.8	495.5	545.6	569.8	628.7
60+	138.2	153.1	169.9	178.8	181.2	190.3	172.3	182.0	183.8	193.5
Subtotal	2,364.9	2,369.0	2,714.5	2,672.8	3,324.8	3,328.9	2,890.4	2,800.5	3,502.2	3,458.5
Total	**4,732.9**		**5,387.3**		**6,653.7**		**5,690.9**		**6,960.7**	

Sources: *ESIA team elaboration based on IHSES 2007 and 2012; **ShelterCluster and CCCM Cluster Rapid Assessment, September 10, 2014 (with REACH); ***UNHCR Registration Trends for Syrian Refugees.
Note: IDPs = internally displaced persons.

Changes in Aggregate and Economic Sector GDP

Official or nonofficial information is available about the KRI gross regional product (GRP) is scarce. Most estimates presented in this section come from consultations with the country counterparts and experts. Thus, results must be considered with caution. The first caveat of these inputs is that the information is available only in current prices. In other words, GRP numbers are not corrected by inflation given the lack of a regional GDP deflator. Even where there is information about the evolution of regional consumption prices, two main reasons can be given not to use them to deflate the GDP: the first is that it is conceptually incorrect given that these indices are not general enough to capture the variation of all types of prices such as those faced by producers in different stages of the production process. The second is the lack of CPI projections for 2015.

Translating Changes in GDP into Changes in Employment

To assess the household-level adjustment to macroeconomic changes on the labor market, the output growth estimates have to be translated into employment changes at the aggregate and sectoral levels. In the absence of a computable general equilibrium or macroeconomic model that predicts these labor market structures, we assume that changes in labor market conditions are proportional to changes in outputs, based on the estimated past relation between output and employment (table 2.14). In other words, this requires estimating sectoral and total output-employment elasticities, which can then be applied to the output growth projections to generate changes in employment by sector and aggregate for any projected year. This implicitly assumes stable relationships between output, demand for labor, and labor earnings, which may not hold because of distortions in the labor market (such as segmentation and downward stickiness of nominal wages) that typically exist in this market and are likely to affect adjustments over time.

Employment by sector is relatively inelastic to changes in sectoral GDP. One set of elasticities is estimated using information on sectoral GDP and employment changes during 2007–12, based on GDP actual data and employment changes for each sector during that period and calculated as the percentage change in employment in the sector between years $t-1$ and t in response to a 1 percent change in sector output for the same period. The findings show that employment is inelastic to changes in GDP (table 2.15). For instance, the agriculture sector would increase its employment by 4 percent for an increase of 1 percent in sectoral GDP.

TABLE 2.14
KRI GRP Growth, by Sector, Estimates

Economic Activity	2007 (ID, billions)	Share (%)	2012 (ID, billions)	Share (%)	Annual Growth Rate
Agriculture	607	6.0	7,040	27.0	63.3
Industry	1,562	15.4	9,386	36.0	43.1
Services	7,983	78.6	9,647	37.0	3.9
Total	**10,152**	**100.00**	**26,074**	**100.0**	**20.8**
Share of Iraq's GDP	19.2		31.1		

Source: ESIA team estimates.

TABLE 2.15
KRI Employment-Output Elasticities (Estimates), Population between 18 and 60 Years
thousands

Economic Activity	Employment					
	2007	Share (%)	2012	Share (%)	Annual Growth Rate	Output Elasticity of Labor
Agriculture	88	10.2	100	8.6	2.7	0.04
Industry	166	19.3	213	18.3	5.2	0.12
Services	606	70.5	851	73.1	7.0	1.82
Total	**860**		**1,164**			

Source: ESIA team estimations based on IHSES 2007 and 2012.

These types of results are not surprising given the weak linkages found between employment and growth in Iraq over the past five-year period.[10]

Changes in Nonlabor Income Components

All nonlabor income components are grouped into two major categories: public and private transfers.[11] Given a lack of information about how these two groups of nonlabor income components are going to be impacted in 2014 and 2015, it is assumed that total public transfers will remain constant over the period, whereas private transfers will be moving according to the growth rate of the total economy. Transfers are not added to or removed from recipient households.

Changes in Prices: Inflation

All household and individual incomes from labor and nonlabor sources are expressed in real terms. However, macroeconomic changes replicated on the microsimulation assume they are in current terms, which implies that poverty estimations are not consistent if a significant change in prices has been seen over the projected years. Given no available projections for the food and nonfood component for KRI for 2015, constant movement in the poverty line is assumed.

Estimating the Welfare Impact of the Shocks, 2012–15

Elasticity of Poverty to Economic Growth

Impact is calculated by using the output–poverty elasticity approach. The elasticity approach uses historical trends of output and poverty to determine the responsiveness of poverty rates to growth in output (and consumption), which is then combined with macroeconomic projections to estimate the impacts of future reduced growth on poverty. Although this method is easy to implement and serves as a convenient benchmark, it is limited in its predictive capability because it yields only aggregate poverty impacts, with no account of the broader distributional effects. It may also prove deficient in predicting poverty impacts during a macroeconomic event that affects output growth in a way that is not entirely consistent with a country's recent growth experience.

In general in Iraq, poverty reduction has been relatively inelastic to increases in GDP growth. An economic growth rate of 7 to 8 percent per year between 2007 and 2012 was accompanied by only a 4 percentage point decline in national poverty rates. Estimates for KRI's total output are available only in current prices, and so for ease of comparison, output-poverty elasticities for Iraq are estimated using GDP in current prices, which yield an estimate of –0.237, which is fairly low. Many reasons can be given for this low poverty response, which are dealt with in detail in the 2014 Poverty Assessment for Iraq.[12] For KRI, given an even smaller decline in head-count rates during the same period, output-poverty elasticity is also low, –0.307. Thus, this simple method, because of the inherent structure of growth in the economy, and the weak links between economic growth, employment, earnings, and welfare in the country as a whole, imply almost no changes in poverty head-count rates as a result of the twin crises in KRI. These are shown in table 2.16. This simple method does not take into account the broader distributional

TABLE 2.16
Elasticity of Poverty to Economic Growth, 2013–15

Year	Scenario		Annual GDP Growth Rate	GDP Total	Population (thousands)	GDP		Headcount Rate	
						Per Capita	Δ%	Δ%	%
2013		Natural	8	25,142	4,940	5,089.74	3.5	−1.07	3.43
2014		Natural	2.6	25,796	5,158	5,001.43	−1.7	0.53	3.45
		IDPs	2.6	25,796	5,926	4,353.22	−14.5	4.45	3.58
		Syrian	2.6	25,796	5,363	4,810.01	−5.5	1.69	3.49
		T + IDPs + Syrian	2.6	25,796	6,133	4,206.28	−17.4	5.33	3.61
2015	Baseline	Natural	6	27,344	5,387	5,075.62	1.5	−0.46	3.43
		IDPs	6	27,344	6,154	4,443.50	2.1	−0.64	3.56
		Syrian	6	27,344	5,591	4,890.75	1.7	−0.52	3.47
		T + IDPs + Syrian	6	27,344	6,361	4,298.89	2.2	−0.68	3.59
	Lower	IDPs	6	27,344	6,404	4,270.03	−1.9	0.59	3.60
		Syrian	6	27,344	5,621	4,864.65	1.1	−0.35	3.47
		T + IDPs + Syrian	6	27,344	6,641	4,117.63	−2.1	0.65	3.63
	Upper	IDPs	6	27,344	6,654	4,109.59	−5.6	1.72	3.64
		Syrian	6	27,344	5,691	4,804.81	−0.1	0.03	3.49
		T + IDPs + Syrian	6	27,344	6,961	3,928.33	−6.6	2.03	3.68

Source: ESIA team estimations based on GDP growth projections.
Note: IDPs = internally displaced person. T = host community's population.

effects of the large influx in population experienced in KRI, and therefore it is preferred to use the results from the microsimulation exercise.

Simulation Results

The natural rate of population growth is assumed to be the same as the 2007–12 average for KRI as estimated based on the 2007 and 2012 IHSES. Assuming no other major changes in the economy, no movement in poverty is seen in KRI between 2012 and 2013. For 2014, four cases are considered: (1) natural, where the population growth rate is the same as in 2007–12; (2) IDP, increase in population as a result of the IDP influx in addition to natural population growth; (3) Syrian, increase in population as a result of the Syrian refugee influx in addition to natural population growth; and (4) Total, which includes natural population growth, along with the population increases implied by the influx of IDPs and Syrian refugees.

The microsimulation results suggest a large poverty impact of increasing poverty rates from 3.5 percent in 2012 up to 8.1 percent in 2014. By itself, the IDP crisis would have increased poverty head-count rates in KRI by more than 3 percentage points in 2014, from an estimated 3.8 percent to an estimated 7.1 percent. The Syrian refugee crisis, because it involves a smaller population influx, implies a higher head-count rate by 1.6 percentage points relative to the benchmark (i.e., natural). Taken together, the twin crises imply an increase of poverty rates, from 3.8 percent at the natural population growth rate in 2014 to 8.1 percent (table 2.17). For 2015, the simulation considers three scenarios—baseline, where the 2014 situation is expected to continue, and a lower and upper bound, which assume ranges for continued increases in IDPs and Syrian refugees in KRI. On the basis of the scenarios considered, between 8 and 10 percent of the persons living in KRI are estimated to be living below the poverty line in 2015.

Stabilization Costs: The Estimated Costs of Achieving the Without-Crisis Poverty Rate

The poverty gap and the increase in head-count rates together yield an estimate of the amount of resources needed to achieve the without-crisis poverty rates. One advantage of using the simulation approach for estimating the welfare impacts of the twin crises is that the implied poverty gap can also be calculated—the average shortfall from the poverty line for those below the line (assuming a zero shortfall for those above the poverty line), expressed as a percentage of the poverty line. Table 2.18 shows estimates for the average poverty gap in thousands of Iraqi dinars, which when multiplied by the additional poor under each scenario (relative to the natural rate of population growth) give an estimate of the amount of resources necessary on average to bring poverty rates down to the without-crisis level. For 2015, annual stabilization costs for the poverty impacts of the twin crises are estimated to range from about ID 77 billion ($66.5 million) to more than ID 125 billion ($107.8 million) depending on the scenario considered. This is the additional transfer needed to bridge the gap between projected consumption and the poverty line.

TABLE 2.17
Aggregate Impacts on Poverty, Assuming No Growth in Public Transfers, 2012–15

Year	Scenario		Headcount (share)		Poor (thousands)	
			Level	Impact	Population	Impact
2012			3.5		164	
2013		Natural	3.5	0.0	172	8
2014		Natural	3.8		194	
		IDPs	7.1	3.3	419	225
		Syrian	5.4	1.6	290	96
		T + IDPs + Syrian	8.1	4.4	499	305
2015	Baseline	Natural	3.8		204	
		IDPs	6.8	3.0	417	213
		Syrian	5.3	1.5	297	93
		T + IDPs + Syrian	7.6	3.8	484	280
	Lower	IDPs	7.6	3.9	489	285
		Syrian	5.4	1.6	303	99
		T + IDPs + Syrian	9.0	5.2	595	390
	Upper	IDPs	8.7	5.0	582	378
		Syrian	5.5	1.7	313	109
		T + IDPs + Syrian	10.4	6.6	723	518

Source: ESIA team estimations.
Note: IDPs = internally displaced persons; T = host community population.

Social Assistance and Labor

The vulnerability of the inhabitants of KRI to shocks increased because of the influx of Syrian refugees and culminated recently with the IDP crisis instigated by ISIS. Before the crises, despite the turbulent conditions in the surrounding region and most particularly in Iraq, KRI had witnessed a considerable rise in prosperity and development. However, because of instability as a spillover of the Syrian and ISIS crises, an impact has been seen on the livelihoods of the population. If the situation remains the

TABLE 2.18
Stabilization Costs, Assuming No Growth in Public Transfers, 2015

		Headcount		Poor (thousands)		Average Monthly Gap	Annual Stabilization Costs
		Level	Impact	Population	Impact	(ID, thousands)	(ID, millions)
Baseline	IDPs	6.8	3.0	417	213	21.5	54,970
	Syrian	5.3	1.5	297	93	20.3	22,643
Lower	IDPs	7.6	3.9	489	285	22.0	75,310
	Syrian	5.4	1.6	303	99	20.7	24,547
Upper	IDPs	8.7	5.0	582	378	21.7	98,471
	Syrian	5.5	1.7	313	109	20.9	27,193

Source: ESIA team estimations.
Note: IDPs = internally displaced persons.

same or worsens, it is expected that a considerable number of IDPs will try to establish their livelihoods in KRI. This requires looking at integration of IDPs into host communities and monitoring closely their entry into the labor market to avoid increased unemployment and undesired reactions that might lead to social tension in host communities.

Baseline and Preconflict Trends in Social Protection and Labor in KRG

KRG provides a number of social protection programs. Starting with social insurance, KRG provides for a mandatory pension system for the public sector (Ministry of Finance), as well as a mandatory social security scheme for the private sector, administered by the KRG Ministry of Labor & Social Affairs (MOLSA). For employment, MOLSA manages various labor programs, including training and employment support, as well as micro- and small-enterprise lending.

MOLSA is the main agency charged with providing social safety net assistance in KRI. Its cash-transfer social safety net program[13] provides cash transfer categorical targeting to specific groups considered vulnerable (widows, the divorced, the abandoned, minor orphans, the elderly, the disabled or injured, families of detainees, and married undergraduate students). This, however, is not subject to any validation in relation to the poverty line, as per the guidelines of the law. Before 2012, a financial assistance of ID 30,000 per household was given monthly. In 2012 this allowance was increased to ID 150,000 per household (regardless of household size), and a total of 189,426 households are benefiting from both family and disability allowances) (KRG and MOLSA 2013). Table 2.19 highlights the trends in benefiting from social assistance (family and disability are the most prominent allowances in KRI), from 2010 to June 2014.

Variations in the number of beneficiaries were noticed through the years. The allowance was increased from ID 30,000 in 2011 and made effective as of 2012. At the same time, the criteria for disability were modified, allowing the inclusion of a higher number of beneficiaries into the system. These cash transfers to both families and disabled are found to be very fluid in applying clear and defined criteria for selection—thus the need for a restructuring of the system delivery that looks at a more thorough targeting using best practices and introducing the poverty line as a definite criterion for selection, in addition to a well-structured social assessment. Social allowances (both family and disability) constituted 80–86 percent of MOLSA's yearly budget[14] in 2012 and 2013.

Labor Market

Foreign labor inflow into KRI grew in the past few years with increased foreign investments. Access to skilled labor was limited in KRI, and so firms started recruiting foreign labor. Figure 2.7 shows the increase in the foreign labor flow into KRI, which shows a drastic decrease in 2014 as many firms put their work on hold and repatriated their foreign labor because of the crisis.

As a result of an increase in the number of investors, increased economic activity, and public sector employment, the KRI unemployment rate declined from 7.9 percent in 2012 to 6.5 percent in 2013 (table 2.20). However, a high proportion of KRI citizens are employed in the public sector (50.6 percent of the labor force in 2013) (KRSO 2013). This is also reflected in the sectoral composition of the labor market, with services accounting for about three-quarters of employment (see figures 2.8 and 2.9).

Although MOLSA provides a well-diversified set of social protection programs that do fall under the two categories (i.e., family and disability allowances), an increasing need is seen to update not only MOLSA's policies and practices to make them more consistent with international practices, but also to enhance KRG's overall social protection system. For this, and upon the request of KRG, the World Bank will support KRG in undertaking a stocktaking of existing social protection policies and

TABLE 2.19
Family and Disability Allowances, by Governorates, 2010–14

	2010 Type of Allowances		2011 Type of Allowances		2012 Type of Allowances		2013 Type of Allowances		June 2014 Type of Allowances	
	Family	Disability	Family	Disability	Family	Disability	Family	Disability	Family	Disability
Erbil	12,699	4,210	20,925	16,589	23,942	40,723	24,110	20,268	25,999	20,620
Sulaymaniyah	17,417	43,455	21,835	46,123	29,746	39,831	30,662	3,898	31,881	37,257
Dohuk	9,302	7,670	21,997	27,989	15,030	32,838	14,165	35,829	20,904	25,999
Garmian					6,436	10,465	6,729	7,802	6,239	7,768
Total	**39,418**	**55,335**	**64,757**	**90,701**	**75,154**	**123,857**	**75,666**	**67,797**	**85,023**	**91,644**
Yearly budget (dollars, thousands)	56,762	79,682	93,250	130,610	108,222	178,354	108,959	97,628		
Estimated additional Households till Dec. 2014									5,101	7,658
Estimated total 2014									129,779	142,995

85

FIGURE 2.7
Foreign Labor Inflow to KRI

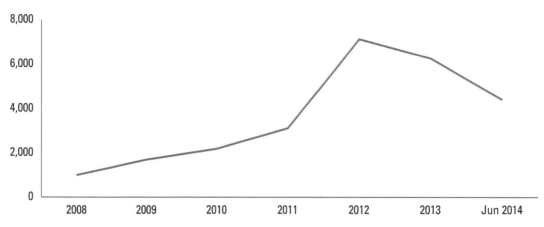

Source: KRG Ministry of Labor and Social Affairs, General Directorate of Labor and Social Insurance, 2014.

TABLE 2.20
Employment and Unemployment Rates, 2012 and 2013

	2012	2013
Labor force (employed and unemployed)	1,196,701	1,339,687
Working-age population (labor force and out of labor)	3,118,394	3,335,741
Total population (working age and non–working age)	4,909,884	5,194,732
Employment rate (%)	35.3	37.5
Unemployment rate (%)	7.9	6.5

Sources: KRSO 2012 and 2013.

programs and develop a KRG Social Protection Strategic Framework (KRG SPSF) consistent with international practices and grounded within the socioeconomic context of KRG. The objective of the KRG SPSF will be to establish a framework for social protection policies and programs that will bring more equity in KRI living standards, thus reducing vulnerability.

Impact of the Syrian Refugees and Iraqi IDPs

KRI has suffered since 2006 from repeated waves of families fleeing conflict both in Iraq and in Syria. The first major inflow came from

FIGURE 2.8
Size of the Labor Force, by Private-Public Sector, 2011–13

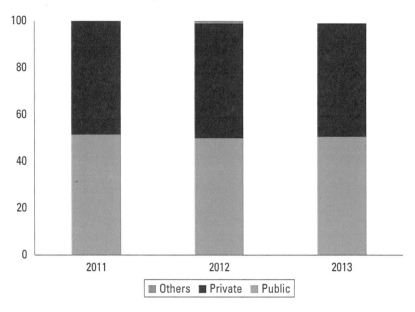

Sources: KRSO 2012 and 2013.

FIGURE 2.9
Labor Force, by Sector, 2012 and 2013

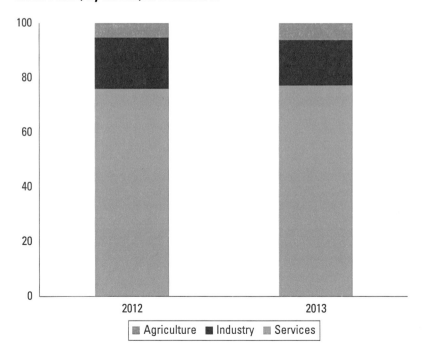

Sources: KRSO 2012 and 2013.

Syria, from where people entered KRI seeking assistance and shelter. These were accommodated at first and were able to adjust and adapt into the community. KRG was able to provide assistance with support from UN agencies and others. However, the situation escalated further with the incoming of the internally displaced population from Iraq in waves as a result of the ISIS crisis. With this recent crisis, KRG has had major challenges of responding to it, which paralleled a financial shock hitting KRG in lack of fiscal transfers from the federal government in Baghdad. The inflow of such a large population of Syrian refugees and Iraqi IDPs would be highly destabilizing. Destabilization could be felt by the pressure that IDPs will exert socially on host communities and on services, and most importantly in the labor market.

MOLSA provides family and disability allowances to enrolled households (HHs). The major obstacle is the absence of fiscal transfers from Baghdad, causing considerable delays in settling the allowances of those in need. It is expected that by end of 2014 the number of beneficiaries from family allowances reached 90,124 HHs, requiring a total of $130 million, and the number of allowances needed for disability would reach 99,302 HHs, requiring $143 million.

It is estimated that 95 percent of refugees in camps reported being able to afford the cost of meeting their basic needs as opposed to 70 percent outside camps.[15] That is why the Syrian inflow was well absorbed by the authorities, who offered all the needed assistance in light of the availability of funds, which is not the case now. As with illegal labor from Iraq and Turkey, many Syrian refugees brought skills to the KRI that are in demand from local employers, and they are also more willing than the local population to work for lower wages. The situation is expected to be different with IDPs arriving with a depletion of social capital. IDPs will be dependent on transfers, assistance, and informal employment arrangements, which might cause strain among the local population.

Reports tell of widespread unemployment. In July and August 2014, foreign firms evacuated foreign labor because of the prevailing security environment. Wages are expected to decline as more IDPs and refugees are entering the labor market. Monitoring the situation remains of great importance to be able to reflect any change in the supply and demand of labor as more IDPs will start seeking livelihoods if the security situation does not improve. The direct impact would lead to an increase in the number of households in need of social safety net assistance.

The fiscal impact will be further compounded as KRG moves to implement the Federal Social Protection Law, enacted in early 2014. On the basis of the poverty impact assessment contained in this report, which estimates that poverty rates will double from 3.5 percent to 8.1 percent,

TABLE 2.21
Fiscal Impact, 2015

	Number of Households	KRG Policies (dollars, millions)	Federal Law (dollars, millions)
Baseline scenario			
Current spending	189,426	273	764
Impact of crisis	116,965	83	231
Total	306,391	356	995
Low case scenario			
Current spending	189,426	273	764
Impact of crisis	150,895	106	296
Total	340,321	379	1,060
High case scenario			
Current spending	189,426	273	764
Impact of crisis	190,898	134	376
Total	380,324	407	1,140

the fiscal impact on the cash transfer social safety net will be substantial. Two scenarios are presented below, to include stabilization at the existing household transfer amount of ID 150,000/month (KRG policies) as well as the average household transfer amount of ID 420,000/month proposed in the Federal Social Protection Law of Iraq. Table 2.21 presents the baseline, the low case, and the high case scenarios for 2015.

Stabilization Needs

Over the short term, livelihood strategies can provide income and reduce tension between IDPs, refugees, and the host community. KRI has many vulnerable households as a result of multiple crises. Community development projects could be initiated where the host community would feel the impact of the project, and IDPs could benefit from cash for work. Projects could be designed to target future needed projects that fall within the national plans of the various sectors. As for the labor aspects, active labor programs are needed to absorb a larger number of workers.

The federal government had begun the implementation of a new social protection law. The cost for the federal government of Iraq is estimated to reach $288 million for a population of 200,000 HHs at approximately $120 monthly. The new social protection law stipulated an increase in the social allowance to reach, on average, ID 420,000 per HH monthly (table 2.22).

TABLE 2.22
Stabilization Assessment, 2015
dollars, millions

		Stabilization Cost (allowance at ID 150,000)		Stabilization Cost (allowance at ID 420,000)	
		Dollars (millions)	Total dollars (millions)	Dollars (millions)	Total dollars (millions)
Baseline[a]	Host community	273		764	
	Syrian refugees	25	356	69	995
	IDPs	58		162	
Low scenario[b]	Host community	273		764	
	Syrian refugees	28	379	79	1,060
	IDPs	78		217	
High scenario[c]	Host community	273		764	
	Syrian refugees	37	407	103	1,140
	IDPs	97		273	

Note: IDPs = internally displaced persons.
a. Status quo—the current population of Syrian refugees and IDPs remains unchanged.
b. Additional influx of 30,000 Syrian refugees and 250,000 Iraqi IDPs.
c. Additional influx of 100,000 Syrian refugees and 500,000 Iraqi IDPs.

Housing and Shelter

Adequate shelter needs to be provided immediately to more than 243,000 vulnerable IDPs. Providing adequate shelter for such a large population has proven an immense challenge for both KRG and the international humanitarian community. The government has built 26 IDP camps across the three governorates of KRI with a total combined capacity for hosting 223,790 IDPs. KRG has committed to funding three of these 26 camps, and the international community is expected to fund 20 camps. The remaining three camps remain unfunded (SEINA-UNDP 2012a, b; United Nations and KRG Ministry of Planning 2014a, b).

The stabilization costs for sheltering IDPs are estimated at $111.3 million.[16] The stabilization cost comprises the cost of establishing three unfunded camps. Under alternative scenarios, which assume a greater influx of refugees and IDPs in 2015, these estimates would rise to $194.6 million under the low scenario and $277.9 million under the high scenario.[17]

Significant resources will also be needed to expand the camp capacity for the Syrian population should the conflict in Syria force more individuals to seek refuge in KRI. Under the low population scenario, which supposes an additional influx of 30,000 Syrian refugees in 2015, and assuming that 40 percent of the population will need to be sheltered in camps, the cost would amount to $10 million. Under the high population scenario, which supposes an additional influx of 100,000 Syrian refugees in 2015 and assuming the same share of population living in camps, the cost would climb to $33 million.

An adverse impact is also associated with 60 percent of the displaced families living in host communities, which is exerting upward pressure on rents and increasing the vulnerability of poor households. An estimated 25,000 IDP households and another 15,000 Syrian families are currently renting accommodations.

Precrisis Situation

With an annual housing demand of almost 60,000 and little provision of affordable housing for low-income households, the housing market in KRI was already under pressure before the IDP and refugee inflow. An estimated 845,000 Kurdish Iraqi HHS were put forward in 2012,[18] a number that according to the KRSO is expected to grow by 4 percent per year. On the basis of these numbers, KRG and UNHABITAT have estimated that the annual housing requirement to accommodate this population growth is 30,390 units across all income levels. In addition, another 25 percent of existing households will require new or improved housing to replace inadequate or overcrowded housing. This equates to 228,000 housing units across all income levels for the next 10 years. Annual housing demand is therefore 53,239 units.

Annual demand for government supported housing is 5,324 units. According to one government study, about 10 percent of households are estimated to have limited incomes to the extent of not being able to meet their housing needs without government support. Limited-income families inhabit approximately 113,170 of existing housing units, and the annual demand for social housing would accordingly be 5,324 units.

Impact of the Crisis

Providing shelter for the most vulnerable displaced families is an urgent concern. The UN seeks to provide winterization kits to vulnerable IDP families. Figure 2.10 presents shelter trends for IDP families between June and September 2014.

FIGURE 2.10
Shelter Trends for IDPs in KRI, June 25, 2014, to September 28, 2014

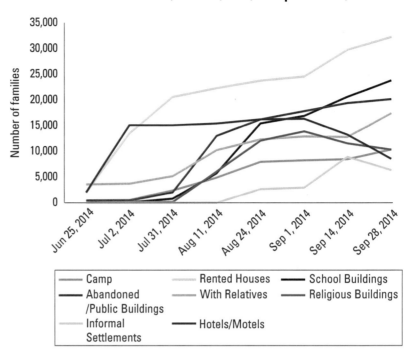

Source: IOM 2014.

More than half of the Syrian refugee population is currently residing outside of camps in host communities. Of these, the large majority (70 percent) live in independent houses or apartments, and a quarter of the total share primarily with other Syrian families. A recent study found that the majority of households found their accommodations to be adequate, although less so in Dohuk than in Erbil and Sulaymaniyah. A substantial number of those reporting inadequate conditions resided in incomplete, dilapidated, and/or poorly constructed buildings or structures. The survey also found that the Syrian population in rented accommodations is finding it increasingly difficult to afford their rent, and rental support was relayed as the most important need for 43 percent of respondents, and among the top three for 68 percent of respondents.

The large number of displaced people settling in rental accommodations will result in rent hikes. Going forward, rents are also expected to rise faster than the overall consumer price index, especially in Dohuk. The additional inflow of 40,000 families currently looking for accommodations will push rent prices upward. The increase in demand for rental accommodations would disproportionately affect the poor in the host community. A large part of the displaced would be competing for accommodations affordable to the 10 percent of the KRI population that is estimated to be in the low to very low income bracket. Using existing poverty levels for Iraqis and Syrians as an indicator for the proportion that would target the lower cost options, the low-income resident households would have to compete with an additional 25,000, 30,000 or 38,000 families, equivalent to a 21, 27, and 33 percent increase, respectively, from the existing low-income resident numbers depending on the inflow scenario (figure 2.11).

Home ownership may mitigate the impact of rent hikes on the host community. Only 13 percent of the KRI population rent their accommodations (and only 10 percent in Dohuk compared with 17 percent and 12 percent in Erbil and Sulaymaniyah, respectively). Although disaggregated data on the share of individuals living in rental accommodations across income quintiles are not available, it would be reasonable to assume that vulnerable groups—such as the poor or female-headed households, which made up 11.6 percent of households in 2012—are the ones relying on rental accommodations and benefiting from the mitigation on rent hikes from the large proportion of homeowners.

FIGURE 2.11
CPI Indicators for Rent and General Prices, January 2012 to January 2015

Source: KRSO.

Stabilization Needs

The stabilization costs for shelter are estimated at $111.3 million based on a cost of providing shelter in camps of $833 per capita and a population in need of shelter of 133,554 individuals. The government has built 26 IDP camps across the three KRI governorates with a total combined capacity for hosting 223,790 IDPs. KRG has committed to funding three of these 26 camps. The international community is expected to fund 20 camps. The remaining three camps are unfunded. The stabilization cost comprises the cost of establishing these three unfunded camps—with a capacity for hosting 25,992 IDPs—as well as providing shelter to the remaining population in need of shelter of 107,562. The World Bank's targeted IDP population in need of shelter is consequently 133,554. Under alternative scenarios, which suppose a greater influx of IDPs in 2015 and 40 percent of which would need a shelter, these estimates would rise to $194.6 million under the low scenario and $277.9 million under the high scenario.

Significant resources will also be needed to expand the camp capacity for the Syrian population should the conflict in Syria force more individuals to seek refuge in KRI. Under the low population scenario, which supposes an additional influx of 30,000 Syrian refugees in 2015, and assuming that 40 percent of the population seeks shelter in camps,[19] the cost would amount to $10 million. Under the high population scenario, which supposes an additional influx of 100,000 Syrian refugees in 2015, and assuming the same share of population living in camps, the cost would climb to $33 million. It should be noted that humanitarian assistance, herein shelter, targeting refugees tends to be better funded by the international community than assistance for IDPs. However, given the scale of the current crisis, the UN is struggling to mobilize the required funding to finance the needs identified in their Regional Response Plan (also covering other Syrian refugee-hosting countries).

Although it is costly for KRG to accommodate the displaced in camps, there are also significant hidden costs to host communities when the displaced find their own housing solutions outside of the camps. Even if all 26 camps are established, this will cover only 30 percent of the existing IDP population. If additional camps were to be established for the remaining population of IDPs in need of shelter, it is estimated that about 45 percent of the IDP population would be living in camps. Communities in KRI are therefore likely to continue to host a large proportion of both Syrian refugees and IDPs. A settlement ratio of 40 percent in camps and 60 percent in host communities would imply that 107,000, 135,000 or 187,000 displaced households would be entering the housing market until the end of 2015 under the baseline, low, and high scenarios for population estimates, respectively. Most of these new entrants would be added to the rental market (figure 2.12).

Increasing the supply of affordable housing for residents could ease prices on the rental market. According to the government strategy on affordable housing, the average annual budgetary provision for housing projects rarely covers more than 10 percent of the annual housing need, with an assumption that the investment in lower-income housing is even lower. Underinvestment is already seen in housing for the poor, so one measure to ease the pressure on the housing market in the medium to long term would be to move forward some of the investments already envisioned in the Ministry of Construction and Housing's strategy to address low-income housing in KRI. At $30,000 per unit, the current goal of building 6,000 government-supported housing amounts to $180 million per year. Although these housing options may not be made available to the displaced populations, they would increase the supply of affordable accommodations in this income strata of the market and lower rents for all.

The increased population pressures also highlight the need to move forward on other aspects of the KRI housing strategy. Government

FIGURE 2.12
Estimated Number of Households Requiring Noncamp Housing in 60/40 Scenario
thousands

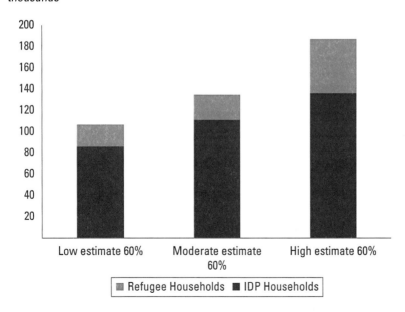

Source: World Bank estimates.
Note: Based on an estimated average household size of six for both refugees and IDPs.
IDPs = internally displaced persons.

provision of housing is not the only tool that can be used to increase the access to affordable housing. KRG has identified actions such as a land development program to make more land available, thereby reducing informal settlements. Also, better access to housing financing and involving private investors in the construction of lower-cost housing would also contribute to medium to longer-term access to and affordability of housing for the poor.

Social Cohesion and Citizen Security

The level of resilience in KRI has been remarkable so far. The hospitality demonstrated by the Iraqi Kurds has been further facilitated by the fact that the peak influx was only a few months ago and the host communities have therefore been largely insulated from direct impacts of the increased population. A main concern for host communities and the displaced relates to security, whether externally or internally instigated, and women have been particularly vulnerable to violence. It is possible that risks of significant deterioration in the relationship between hosts and displaced might emerge, likely stemming from mounting socioeconomic pressure on host communities, the prevalence of conflict-related stress such as trauma and frustration, and the threat of domestic security incidents.

The lack of security contributes to recurrent cycles of fragility while also imposing an additional burden on state building and public finance.[20] As the 2011 World Development Report suggests, weakened resilience, coupled with an erosion of confidence in government, poor access to services, and underemployment, raises social risk and constitutes the core of new understandings of state fragility (World Bank 2011b). Social isolation, discrimination by local populations, strained social welfare services, and poor access to basic services also contribute to an erosion of economic status and security. The prospects for displaced women-headed households to escape poverty and to better their living conditions are particularly grim (Cohen 2000). Stresses such as these not only contribute to conflict and fragility, but also reflect challenges for key national institutions to deal with citizen security, justice, and development.[21]

Precrisis Situation

The KRI population has a long history of themselves being and receiving refugees. Most long-time residents of KRI are able to cite family members lost or displaced over the previous 40 years and direct experience with forced displacement as well. Iraqi Kurds have also regularly hosted refugee populations from other countries. Several populations are in protracted exile in KRI, including 10,000 Iranian Kurds from 1979, more than 5,000 non-Kurd Iranian refugees from 1982, and 3,000–5,000 Turkish refugees as of 1998. An additional 10,000–15,000 internally displaced Iraqis are in the three governorates of KRI from the waves of internal displacement that originated in central and southern Iraq in 2003–8.

Violence in the KRI has remained low for many years, indicating both a high level of internal security and social cohesion not found in the rest of Iraq. Not only does the KRI score significantly higher on the Economist Intelligence Unit internal peace index, but the region is also in the top for the MENA region as a whole. However, gun ownership is widespread, a culturally accepted practice facilitated by the ease with which people can obtain a weapon without a permit (figure 2.13).

Citizen security is furthermore bolstered by low levels of reported crime, including those related to property. The reported incidents of theft are very low by international standards, although these figures likely reflect a significant level of underreporting. That being said, the reported figures are supported by widespread perceptions of low crime levels by both residents and foreigners.

FIGURE 2.13
Monthly Civilian Deaths by Violence, January 1, 2009, through September 1, 2013
million inhabitants

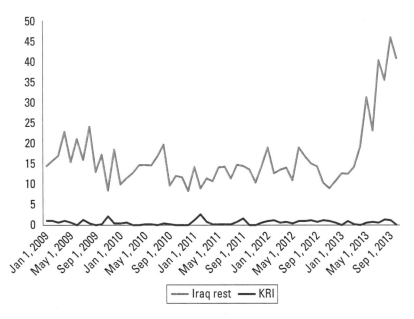

Source: Iraq Body Count Database 2014 World Bank data.

Expenditures related to internal security have slowly declined since 2012. Public expenditures for internal security (primarily police and military police) went up significantly in 2009, even before the onset of the Syrian crisis. Per capita spending for recurrent costs has doubled from 2009 to 2011.[22] Since 2012, the relative share of security spending by KRG declined.

Impact Assessment on Social Cohesion and Citizen Security

Host communities are adversely affected by the crisis. The added burden of inflows has delayed the school year and prompted water shortages in Dohuk, created wage and rental price distortions throughout KRI, and caused delivery deficits to emerge in health care in host areas (United Nations Office for the Coordination of Humanitarian Affairs 2014a). UNDP highlighted the importance of taking actions to clear schools that are occupied by IDPs, improve shelter options, and address service delivery deficits. UNHCR/REACH data suggest that a population of 410,969 in host communities[23] are adversely affected by refugee and IDP inflows as a result of proximity to concentrations of forcibly displaced populations (United Nations Office for the Coordination of Humanitarian Affairs 2014b).

The KRG authorities and host communities have demonstrated extensive generosity and openness in supporting the Syrian refugees. Most Iraqi Kurds of all ages have vivid memories of being displaced themselves, many of them multiple times, and the empathy and understanding of the plight of forced displacement is therefore widespread and deep-rooted. The fact that a majority of the Syrian refugees are ethnic Kurds has further facilitated the integration of this group into KRI society, supported by an appreciation of the quality of the skilled labor that many of the Syrians bring into the economy. It has thus been relatively easy for the Syrian refugees to obtain the local registration cards that allow them to work legally in the country.

Initially IDPs settled along ethnic and confessional lines where possible. This has helped mitigate social tensions and has provided a stronger support network for the incoming groups. However, overcrowding is becoming a major problem in certain areas in the cities such as in Dohuk and Erbil governorates, and vulnerability is now heightened among ethnic minorities with few or no established links with the host communities, people living in unfinished or abandoned buildings, or those living in the open as well as those living in overcrowded conditions.

Hospitality and generosity has also been extended to the IDPs arriving from southern Iraq, although the confessional diversity and previous history of adversity make the relationship somewhat more complicated. As with the Syrian refugees, local families have opened their homes and organized the collection of donations, supported by the private and public sector.

However, the risk of tensions might increase in mixed camp environments and host communities. Experience from other displacement settings shows that social tensions among communities of IDPs might occur, especially in mixed camps. The ISIS crisis is more recent, and so host communities have not experienced the full impact on their livelihoods yet. However, experience from neighboring countries shows that in the long term a large influx of displaced populations risks contributing to increases in prices for basic commodities and rents, while an increasing supply of labor results in a downward pressure on wages, all of which can dampen tolerance and hospitality.

Recommendations for Stabilization

In the current crisis environment, KRG is facing serious challenges. Looking at experience from other displacement situations, insulating the host communities to the extent possible from adverse impacts on their quality of life will remain a priority to minimize tensions. This entails investment in social service delivery to ensure uninterrupted access to and quality of services, but also in the safeguarding of people's livelihoods and purchasing power. According to the Immediate Response Plan, the cost of security related to hosting IDPs will amount to between $334 and $562 million for 2015.

Strengthening KRG's capacity to manage and coordinate the response to the crisis should be a key priority. A better coordinated approach and risk management capacity would be crucial in minimizing both the probability and the potential impact of the risks. Inspiration could be taken from the realm of disaster risk management, which focuses on developing the capabilities for prevention, coordination, and communication. Risk identification and management would also be a strong tool for KRG in their policy formulation and prioritization of interventions aimed at addressing the crisis.

Such risk management efforts should include tracking of social cohesion deficits. The International Organization for Migration is currently mapping ethnic and sectarian settlement patterns, and UNHCR has begun to collect data on social cohesion, using proxy variables. For actual programming, an early warning system could be used to orient the rapid service delivery initiatives that benefit hosts and the displaced in fragile areas. Immediate efforts need to be made to safeguard the cordial relations between residents and displaced.

To alleviate the pressure on host communities and reduce perceptions of preferential treatment of the displaced, assistance should preferably target both vulnerable host and displaced communities. KRG already has a successful experience of using consultative mechanisms to deliver services in underserved population centers throughout KRI. When coupled with targeting from an early warning system, this may be an appropriate recovery operation to address transitional fragility in the recovery phase.

Notes

1. The World Bank team was unable to collect reliable utilization data for 2011–14.
2. UN internal reports shared with the World Bank team.
3. At the start of the school year in September 2014, more than 750 schools in KRG were used as shelters by IDPs, but this number has declined significantly as other housing solutions have been found for the refugees.
4. The assumptions, scenarios, and data for the displaced are from Jennings (2014).
5. United Nations World Food Program 2014.
6. This baseline per capita estimate is repeated in several reports, including KRG (2014a).
7. World Food Programme, Iraq Revised Strategic Response Program for February–December 2014.
8. It should be noted here that in KRI, poverty (as measured by consumption) has been relatively inelastic to economic growth, so that changes in growth alone will leave poverty unaffected, and that the data on projected GDP and its sectoral composition in KRI are particularly weak.
9. For further details of the methodology see Olivieri et al. (2014).
10. See *The Unfulfilled Promise of Oil and Growth. Poverty, Inclusion and Welfare in Iraq 2007–12*, World Bank Group.
11. Public transfers include pensions, rations, social protection, and other public transfers. Private transfers comprise incomes from capital, remittances (domestic and international), *zakat,* and other private transfers.
12. See *The Unfulfilled Promise of Oil and Growth. Poverty, Inclusion and Welfare in Iraq 2007–12*, World Bank Group.
13. Social safety nets are defined by the World Bank as noncontributory transfers targeted to the poor or vulnerable. They include income support, temporary employment programs (workfare), and social services that build human capital and expand access to finance among the poor and vulnerable. If well designed and implemented, social safety nets can build resilience to crisis by helping households navigate the effects of shocks.
14. Information from the General Directorate of Budgeting, Ministry of Finance and Economy, KRG.
15. "Comparative Analysis of Syrian Refugees Staying Inside and Outside Camps in Kurdistan Region of Iraq," UNHCR, September 2014. http://reliefweb .int/report/iraq/comparative-analysis-syrian-refugees-staying-and-outside -camps-kurdistan-region-iraq
16. This is based on the assumption of a cost of providing shelter of $833 per person. This cost does not include the cost of providing security for camps. Other costs associated with the securitization of the camp are inevitable, but these are beyond the scope of this assessment.
17. This is based on the assumption that 40 percent of the additional population of refugees and IDPs will be in need of shelter.

18. According to the 2012 Iraq Household Socioeconomic Survey.
19. This assumes that the sociodemographic profile of the additional influx of Syrian refugees and IDPs will remain unchanged. This is consistent with the existing settlement pattern seen among Syrian refugees in KRI and in Jordan.
20. This is the case not only in Iraq, but also in other, parallel displacement crises found in Afghanistan, Azerbaijan, the Democratic Republic of Congo, Sudan, and multiple venues in Europe and Central Asia. See, for example, De Berry and Petrinin (2011); World Bank (2011a), and World Bank and UNHCR (2011).
21. World Bank. "Operationalizing the WDR." World Bank, Washington, DC. http://siteresources.worldbank.org/DEVCOMMINT/Documentation/22884392 /DC2011-0003(E)WDR2011.pdf
22. The assessment focused on those areas more directly associated with the delivery of security services: the General Directorate of Police, the General Directorate of the Zervani (military police), the General Directorate for Combating Violence against Women, and the Office for Migration and Displacement.
23. Host communities are defined as population living within a 2 kilometer radius of IDP and refugee.

CHAPTER 3

Impact of the Conflict on Infrastructure

The refugee and ISIS crises increased stress on KRI's infrastructure, which was already facing challenges. For example, the crises are adding more stress on an already existing ailing system of solid waste management. An average of 2.5 to 3.5 kilograms of solid waste is generated by in-camp refugees and IDPs, and 1.2 kilograms for IDPs and refugees living in regular housing dwellings. This added population produced more than 1,690 tons of solid waste per day, an increase of 26 percent over KRI daily per capita generated solid waste in 2014. In terms of capacity for absorbing solid waste, it appears that only Dohuk City is ready to continue to accept additional solid waste because of the construction of a new sanitary landfill and because of its current capacity for recycling. It is expected that in 2015 onward, the following interventions in solid waste management in KRI would be required: (1) the closure and rehabilitation of open and uncontrolled municipal solid waste dumps, especially in Erbil and Sulaymaniyah; (2) establishing composting, separating, and landfilling facilities, especially in Erbil, which has no waste-recycling activities; and (3) locating appropriate land and construction of a new sanitary landfill to serve Sulaymaniyah City and surroundings.

Furthermore, water demand is increasing in KRI, and the sanitation situation is a concern, especially in the camps. Water supply and sanitation systems were already facing challenges before the crises in providing continuous service to the KRI population. Although the proportion of the population using improved access to water is above 90 percent, the quality of service remains poor. The sharp increase in access to water supply services has not been accompanied by similar investments in wastewater infrastructure. Sanitation remains a major concern, most notably in camps. Between October 2012 and September 2014,

PHOTO 3.1
Gawilan Refugee Camp in Dohuk Governorate

Gawilan refugee camp profile in Dohuk governorate, November 2014. The tents that are nearest were placed directly on the ground in an immediate response to the influx of Kobani refugees at that time. The remaining camps in the background are part of the permanent camp where refugees have tents on concrete bases to protect the tents from the harsh elements as well as families having access to their own kitchen and washing facilities. © UNHCR/T. Tool. Used with the permission of UNHCR/T. Tool; further permission required for reuse.

the additional demand for water for refugees and IDPs is estimated at 11 percent. The stabilization costs for 2015 range between $214.3 million and $347.7 million across the baseline and high scenarios.

The refugee and IDP crises had an impact on domestic energy demand and prices. Gasoline prices increased to ID 900 per liter, and the price for diesel doubled to ID 950 per liter in June 2014. These sharp increases have impacted economic activities. The electricity sector is heavily dependent on government support: The Ministry of Finance transferred ID 80 billion each month in 2013. The tariff level and collection rates are insufficient to cover operating costs and capital expenditures. Demand is increasing: For example, the electricity network demand load in Erbil reached its peak in August 2014 through a 22 percent increase compared with August 2013. In Sulaymaniyah, additional capacity of 125 megawatts is needed. For IDPs the cost of installing a low-voltage electricity network is estimated at about ID 500–700 million for each medium-size camp.

Water and Sanitation Sector

Background: Water and Sanitation Sector in KRI

Water supply and sanitation systems were already facing challenges before the current crises in providing continuous service to the

KRI population. The proportion of the population using improved access to water is more than 90 percent. The quality of service, however, in terms of continuity of access and water pressure remains poor. Water consumption in KRI is estimated to range between 373 and 400 liters per capita per day. This remains very high relative to the median water consumption of middle-income countries of about 162 liters per capita per day. The high consumption is largely explained by overdesign of the system, which is further aggravated by modest prices.[1] In 2011 expenditures for operations and maintenance (O&M) were $119.2 million, capital investment was $153.5 million, but water fee collection revenues amounted to only $5.2 million.[2] Furthermore, the cost recovery of O&M is only 4.4 percent.

The sharp increase in access to water supply services has not been accompanied by similar investments in wastewater infrastructure. Sanitation remains a major concern, most notably in IDP camps. The major gaps relate to physical facilities, namely, the lack of wastewater treatment plants and sewerage collection networks, except in Sulaymaniyah Governorate. The lack of sanitation increases public health risks and environmental pollution. On the water supply side, the use of groundwater[3] has resulted in lowering of the water table, which results in higher costs to treat and pump the water. Furthermore, a significant gap exists between the rural and urban areas in terms of population with access to improved water sources and sanitation facilities.

The water and sanitation sector needs to improve its efficiency of spending. Despite recurrent and investment budget allocations to the Ministry of Water Resources, the implementation of a coherent investment strategy is difficult because of the lack of an integrated budget and the split in responsibilities of water between ministries. Salaries make up a significant share of the operational budget. Unless the poor collection rates are reversed, even large tariff increases may not compensate for lost revenue. The main causes of poor finances are insufficient tariffs, which do not allow cost recovery to be achieved.

Impact Assessment

The influxes of Syrian refugees and the Iraqi IDPs have exacerbated the challenges that were already present. The additional demand for water increased by 11 percent between October 2012 and September 2014, relative to the precrisis level.

The cumulative fiscal impact from October 2012 to September 2014 is estimated at $33 million, of which $13.3 million is attributable to Syrian refugees and $19.7 million to IDPs. The targeted population of IDPs (United Nations and KRG Ministry of Planning 2014a) in the current

KRG plan is defined as the (1) IDPs living in the open air, (2) IDPs living in schools, churches, and mosques, and (3) IDPs in unfinished buildings. For 2012 and 2013, the impact is reflected in the additional actual capital and O&M expenditure.[4] Given that the budget was not transferred in 2014, the estimated impact was calculated by multiplying the number of out-camp refugees and IDPs (those living in houses, hotels, and with families) by the ratio of planned capital and O&M cost averaged for 2014. International organizations covered about $150 million for emergency and short-term spending on water supply and sanitation. It has also been reported that the private sector (water tankers, sanitation) have significantly increased prices for water and sanitation services (table 3.1).

Stabilization Assessment

The stabilization costs for 2015 range between $214.3 million and $347.7 million across the baseline and high scenarios (see table 3.2). The estimated needs are calculated by estimating the cost of in-camp refugees and IDP and out-camp refugees and IDPs. The cost of in-camp refugees and IDPs was estimated by multiplying the number of in-camp refugees and IDPs by a fixed amount of $40 per month per person.[5] The share of in-camp refugees is estimated at 45 percent, and the share of in-camp IDPs is estimated at 36 percent. This stabilization assessment covers the costs of investment and operations for water supply and sanitation in camps. The cost of out-camp refugees and IDPs was estimated by multiplying the number of out-camp refugees and IDPs by the ratio of projected capital and O&M estimated for 2014.

Solid Waste Management

Solid waste management is a concern with the increased refugee and IDP population. An average of 2.5 to 3.5 kilograms[6] of solid waste was generated by in-camp refugees and IDPs and 1.2 kilograms by IDPs and refugees living in regular housing dwellings.[7] This additional population produced more than 1,690 tons of solid waste per day, an increase of 26 percent over KRI daily per capita generated solid waste in 2014,[8] adding more stress on an already existing ailing system of solid waste management and contributing potentially to air, soil, and groundwater contamination and pollution. In 2014 onward, expenditures on solid waste management in KRI are expected to increase not only because of pressure introduced by the issue of IDPs and refugees, but the capacity of landfilling in the KRI is already stressed with the two major landfills in

TABLE 3.1
Estimated Impact on Water Demand, 2012–14
dollars, millions

	2012	2013	2014 (first 9 months)	
	Actual		**Estimated**	
			Syrian Refugee and Iraqi IDP Influx	
	Syrian Refugee Influx	**Syrian Refugee Influx**	**Syrian Refugee Influx**	**Iraqi IDP Influx**
Impact assessment	4.3	2.6	6.4	19.7
Current spending	4.3	2.6	2.3	7.1
Capital spending	0.0	0.0	4.1	12.6

Sources: Ministry of Water data/discussions and World Bank staff calculations.
Note: IDP = internally displaced person.

TABLE 3.2
Estimated Needs of Refugees and IDPs, 2015 Projection
dollars, millions

	Baseline[a]		Low Scenario[b]		High Scenario[c]	
	Syrian Refugees	**IDPs**	**Syrian Refugees**	**IDPs**	**Syrian Refugees**	**IDPs**
Stabilization (Needs) Assessment	51.8	162.5	58.5	216.7	75.9	271.8
Current spending						
Operations and maintenance needed for stabilization for out-camp	3.1	12.6	3.6	16.9	4.7	21.3
Provision of access of water and sanitation for in-camp	43.2	127.7	48.5	169.8	62.9	213.0
Capital spending						
Capital investment needs for stabilization out-camp	5.5	22.2	6.4	30.0	8.3	37.6

Source: Ministry of Water data and World Bank staff calculations.
Note: IDPs = internally displaced persons.
a. Status quo—the current population of Syrian refugees and IDPs remains unchanged.
b. Additional influx of 30,000 Syrian refugees and 250,000 Iraqi IDPs.
c. Additional influx of 100,000 Syrian refugees and 500,000 Iraqi IDPs.

Sulaymaniyah and Erbil cities scheduled to close by 2016, and the occurrence of illegal and open dumping and burning (for instance, Erbil Governorate has more than 75 open dumping sites).

In terms of capacity for absorbing solid waste, it appears that only Dohuk City is ready to continue to accept additional solid waste because of the construction of a new sanitary landfill that is ready and because of its current capacity for recycling (only 25 percent of Dohuk City daily generated solid waste goes for landfilling).[9] Except in municipalities and other local KRI government administrations that manage solid waste collection and disposal using their own staff, initial feedback shows that the cost for solid waste collection generated by the influx of IDPs and refugees has not changed dramatically between 2012 and 2014, because private sector solid waste collection contractors are bound with three-year contracts for a fixed annual rate. It is expected that in 2015 onward, the following interventions in solid waste management in the KRI would be required (not factoring in stabilization analysis): (1) the closure and rehabilitation of open and uncontrolled municipal solid waste dumps, especially in Erbil and Sulaymaniyah; (2) establishing composting, separating, and landfilling facilities, especially in Erbil, which has no waste recycling activities; and (3) locating appropriate land and construction of a new sanitary landfill to serve Sulaymaniyah City and surroundings (population of 725,000).[10] A report prepared by UNDP and KRG Ministry of Planning (2012) estimates that $352 million of investments in solid waste treatment and disposal would be required between 2013 and 2018, with expectations that a high proportion of this amount ($250.4 million) would need to be invested by the end of 2015 (out of which $197.5 million would be invested by the private sector). Furthermore, financial support would need to be extended to the host communities for two reasons.

First, the governorates of Erbil, Dohuk, and Sulaymaniyah heavily rely on the private sector to collect, treat, and transfer solid waste to landfilling and dumping sites. The local government responsibilities are limited to covering solid waste and monitoring and inspecting the private sector performance. In 2011 it is estimated that the operating expenditure spent on private sector contracts was $42.7 million,[11] about 84 percent of total expenditures (capital and recurrent) on solid waste management in the three governorates. The majority of private sector contracts, having a life of three years, are scheduled to expire by the end of 2014. Any new contracts signed are expected to factor for the additional cost associated with the additional solid waste generated by the influx of refugees and IDPs. In addition, some municipalities, Erbil municipality, for instance, have had to sign new contracts with the private sector for the collection and transfer from some camps that are no longer served by the UN for solid waste management.

Second, once permanent[12] camps are established for refugees and IDPs, the responsibility for solid waste collection and transfer is expected to be transferred from the UN to the host local governments.

Solid Waste Management in the Precrisis Conditions

KRI's local governments are characterized by a high dependence on central government transfers and a weak revenue base to sustain vital local government services. Solid waste management is no exception. Particularly for this service, KRI municipalities and other local governments do not charge citizens for garbage collection and disposal. Per capita expenditure for solid waste management is about $13.[13] Local governments charge fines for illegal road dumping, if spotted, and without applying serious law enforcement measures. Investment needs for waste recycling and sanitary landfilling exceed the available resources.

The ratio of urban areas served in solid waste management to those rural areas is dramatically different (with service coverage reaching 100 percent in city centers) because municipal institutions are not responsible for services outside the municipal boundaries based on the Municipalities Administrative Law (165) of 1964 (Iraq Ministry of Planning and Central Statistical Organization 2013). According to the KRG Ministry of Planning (2013) more than 40 percent of rural households report disposing their garbage in open areas, and 18 percent report burning or burying their garbage. Comparatively, more than 95 percent of solid waste of urban areas is collected and disposed of using landfilling. This decreases the percentage of population served with this service in the rural areas, where random and open space dumping is usual and visible. Even before the demand generated by the influx of IDPs and refugees, open dumping and waste burning were common practices across KRI. Large dumping sites are available for waste generated by large cities, and smaller municipalities and local governments revert to dumping in small landfills and open areas. Disposal of solid waste in small and large sites alike is characterized by suboptimal burning and covering practices that do not meet minimum sanitary landfilling and solid waste disposal standards. All sorts of solid waste (domestic, commercial, construction, industrial, and other including hospital waste and other hazardous waste) are disposed of "conveniently." This increases the risk of diseases and contamination through air and water pollution, and through direct human contact with waste, including untreated hospital and other hazardous waste.

The Environmental Law is not enforced. General neglect or avoidance of environmental impact assessments is seen for most public and private projects, making it difficult to manage or reduce the environmental impacts of large projects. Hardly any attempts (except for a recycling project in Dohuk and a waste-to-electricity project, both managed by the private sector through payments from the local governments) are made to recycle solid waste or dispose of it under sanitary conditions that would minimize the environmental impact. That more than 60 percent of solid waste generated in the KRI is organic waste[14] makes this either an opportunity for composting in cooperation with the private sector or, as it is now, an environmental hazard with levels of methane gas trapped in dangerous quantities because of improper solid waste–covering practices at dumping sites, and with no serious consideration at this stage for landfill methane gas commercial production.

The National Solid Waste Management Plan for the Republic of Iraq was developed in 2007. The plan states that Iraq will build 33 engineered landfills with capacity of 600 million square meters in all of the 18 governorates in Iraq, including Erbil, Dohuk, and Sulaymaniyah governorates, by 2027. In addition to constructing landfills, the plan also focuses on the collection and transportation, recycling, disposal, and reuse systems. In KRI, in 2011, the Ministry of Municipalities and Tourism, in cooperation with UNICEF, prepared a Solid Waste Master Plan for each of the three governorates, taking into consideration proposing waste recovery, reuse, and disposal techniques that were specific for each governorate. The activities in the master plans could be implemented subject to availability of funding. For example, recently a contract was signed by the Ministry of Municipalities and Tourism and a Canadian company to construct two recycling plants on the eastern and western outskirts of Erbil City.

The responsibility for solid waste collection and disposal in the majority of Erbil's 66 municipalities is transferred to the private sector through tendering of contracts. Most contracts are for three years with a total contract amount distributed over monthly payments. The exception to this is 12 small local governments that manage solid waste collection and disposal using their own staff and dispose of solid waste in open dumping areas on the outskirts of these municipalities. Erbil City has a large dumping site (Kani Karzalah) 10 kilometers away from the city center, which is scheduled to close by 2016. A new sanitary landfill is under construction, and another one is also planned together with a waste separation plant. Erbil Governorate has no formal recycling activities, and experts stress that the primary priority for improving solid waste management in Erbil would be by introducing waste separation and recycling initiatives. Since 2011 the municipality of Erbil has announced plans to build recycling plants with various international firms, none of which has materialized thus far. Erbil Governorate produces about 4,300 tons of municipal solid waste per day,[15] and it goes to landfills almost without any treatment or reduction. At this stage, an "informal" community of recyclers composed of waste pickers roams open dumping sites walking around toxic mounds of trash looking for metal and other recyclables.

Impact Assessment

As a result of the refugee and IDP inflows, Erbil's solid waste increased by a little more than 300 tons daily. Even before the crises, the city of Erbil was producing large quantities of untreated solid waste. The system could benefit from improvements, especially through introducing waste separation and recycling schemes in public-private sector partnership. This may include composting (56 percent of Erbil City's[16] waste is organic waste), waste to energy, and gas commercial production. A Solid Waste Master Plan for Erbil Governorate was prepared in 2011 and already has proposals for various potential separation, treatment, and recycling plants in the short and long terms.

Sulaymaniyah City is faced with a major challenge, because no land is available for the proposed new sanitary landfill location. Sulaymaniyah Governorate includes 76 municipalities within 10 districts and 50 subdistricts and many villages. The majority[17] of the governorate's solid waste is managed by the private sector, out of which three contracts are currently signed with Sulaymaniyah City. The main landfill in Sulaymaniyah (Tanjaro) is located approximately 10 kilometers south of Sulaymaniyah City and is nearly saturated. Sulaymaniyah has introduced recycling schemes; for example, an international cement company uses a recycling plant to process between about 1,000 and 1,500 tons of solid waste per day (estimated by Sulaymaniyah City staff to be nearly 60 percent of the city's daily solid waste generated), and the unrecyclable trash is then burned at no harm to the environment to produce energy for the cement factory.

Dohuk is the only governorate in the KRI that can be considered to be the most advanced in terms of use of sanitary and proper solid waste management. Dohuk governorate has 46 municipalities and seven districts, out of which 13 municipalities manage solid waste using their own staff and resources and use open dumping in designated areas on the municipalities' outskirts. Dohuk Governorate has two large sanitary landfills, one of which is relatively new and has a service life of 10 years. Dohuk was also the first city in KRI to invest in recycling, and currently it is estimated that only about 25 percent of Dohuk Governorate's solid waste goes to landfilling; the rest is separated and either recycled locally or sold to foreign companies. Dohuk City hired a foreign firm to build a facility that separates trash into materials that can be recycled, composted, or buried. It has been operating since 2010, processing between 350 and 500 tons of waste a day. The city of Dohuk will be commissioning a new recycling facility, which is estimated to process an additional 500 tons a day.

Aarbad Camp in Sulaymaniyah and Khanki Camp in Dohuk report no serious deterioration in the quality of solid waste management, at least in the near future. For example, both of these camps' directors and residents confirmed that garbage is collected at least twice daily from camps, and they expressed their satisfaction about the quality of services. The main reason for this is likely to be the fact that the UN or host municipalities use the private sector to collect and transfer solid waste from camps. Out of 16 camps for IDPs and refugees in the governorate, only one camp in Dohuk falls outside the jurisdiction of Dohuk Municipality, in Amedi, whose solid waste is managed by the host municipality. It is estimated that in-camp IDPs and refugees are costing either the UN or their host municipalities about $2 per capita per day for cleaning services (United Nations and KRG Ministry of Planning 2014a).

Additional solid waste management and treatment facilities are underway. A new recycling plant in Sulaymaniyah will be operational in 2015, through a contract with the private sector that charges per ton of solid waste treated. The cost of the additional tons of solid waste generated by the additional population (refugees and IDPs) will increase the amount that the private sector will charge Sulaymaniyah Municipality. Currently camps in Sulaymaniyah Governorate are serviced by the UN, including solid waste management through payments to the private sector for the service. Once permanent camps are constructed, the responsibility for solid waste management in the camps will be transferred to the host communities, who need to factor in this additional cost from 2015 onward.

Stabilization Assessment

The stabilization cost for the solid waste management sector is estimated to range between $25.9 million and $42.4 million across the baseline and high scenarios for 2015 (table 3.3).

TABLE 3.3
Stabilization Assessment for Solid Waste Management, 2015 Projection
dollars, millions

	Baseline[a]		Low Scenario[b]		High Scenario[c]	
	Syrian Refugees	IDPs	Syrian Refugees	IDPs	Syrian Refugees	IDPs
Stabilization (needs) assessment	5.9	20.0	6.7	26.9	8.7	33.7
Current spending	3.5	12.0	4.0	16.1	5.2	20.2
Capital spending	2.3	8.0	2.7	10.8	3.5	13.5

Note: IDPs = internally displaced persons.
a. Status quo—the current population of Syrian refugees and IDPs remains unchanged.
b. Additional influx of 30,000 Syrian refugees and 250,000 Iraqi IDPs.
c. Additional influx of 100,000 Syrian refugees and 500,000 Iraqi IDPs.

Electricity Sector

The electricity sector plays a pivotal role in supporting economic growth in KRI. Notwithstanding the considerable infrastructure development in recent years, due to systemic problems, such as the weak financial situation, the need for additional governmental support, and the lack of corporatization and strategic planning, major barriers to the efficient functioning of the sector remain. The migration of Syrian refugees and IDPs to KRI has magnified these challenges and the need to address these issues. The stabilization cost for 2015 is estimated to range between $275 million and $517 million across the baseline and high scenarios for better service delivery.

Background

The electricity sector in KRI is under the jurisdiction of the KRG Ministry of Electricity. The Ministry of Electricity operates as a vertically integrated (generation, transmission, and distribution) electric utility with three distribution directorates in Erbil, Dohuk, and Sulaymaniyah. It owns all transmission and distribution facilities, hydroelectric power plants, and a few older thermal generating plants.

Electricity generation in KRI is largely dominated by the private sector. At present, 95 percent of the generation capacity is privately owned, and 5 percent is government owned. Most generation capacity comes from thermal power plants, and hydroelectric power plants provide a small fraction (about 3–5 percent). The majority of base load thermal generating plants installed during the last 10 years are owned by private companies with contractual power purchase agreements (PPAs). The Ministry of Electricity takes all risks in the power generation sector. KRI supplies fuel for electricity generation to independent power producers; in return, independent power producers supply electricity to the three governorates. All PPAs are based on a take-or-pay provision. Because of increased demand, the independent power producers have commissioned new gas-turbine power plants given KRG's plans to boost natural gas use in power generation (KRG 2012a).

The electricity sector service delivery in the region has recorded important achievements since 2010. The installed generation capacity has more than tripled and reached 3.9 gigawatts, and the electricity supply has almost reached 22 to 24 hours of service. During the same period, power generation has increased by 17 percent on average per year. During the past few years, the electricity consumption in the region has grown significantly. The peak demand for 2013 was 3.5 gigawatts and exceeded the KRG 2009 Electricity Master Plan projections.

However, the sector still faces serious challenges, such as high technical and nontechnical losses, transmission and distribution system bottlenecks, low tariff and collection rates, lack of regulatory frameworks, and high dependence on budgetary support. The total losses of the system are about 35–38 percent, more than half of which is technical and remains high in comparison with international standards. Commercial losses are about 20 percent of the total dispatched energy, which means that a significant portion of electricity generated does not bring any revenues. Several physical infrastructure investments are needed to improve the service quality of the transmission and distribution networks. The governorates of Dohuk, Erbil, and Sulaymaniyah are connected with a transmission network with limited power transfer capability during peak months. However, after the introduction of a 400 kilovolt north-south transmission line, all three governorates will be better interconnected, and the power transfer capability between the regions and neighboring countries could significantly increase.

The electricity sector is heavily dependent on the government's support in terms of financial and operational sustainability. According to the joint report by the KRG Ministry of Planning and UNDP (SEINA) in December 2012 on KRI's infrastructure needs, financial subsidies reached $1.8 billion in 2011, equivalent to 2.8 times the total spending for ongoing projects in the electricity sector and 55 percent of total expenditure in 2011 for ongoing projects in the entire region. Given that the existing tariff level and collection rates are insufficient to cover the operating cost

and capital expenditures, the KRG Ministry of Finance continues to provide financial support to the Ministry of Electricity.[18] The absence of efficient regulatory and institutional schemes, combined with a lack of a
strategic plan, undermines the sector's financial sustainability.

To reduce the fuel cost and improve the financial situation of the
electricity sector, KRG plans to substitute expensive diesel feedstock
with domestically produced natural gas in power plants within the
next two to three years. The natural gas potential is currently being
developed, and new gas pipeline infrastructure is expected to be fully
operational by 2016–17. Some of the completed projects include a
176 kilometer pipeline taking gas from the Khor Mor field to power
plants in Erbil and Sulaymaniyah and to Khurmala and a 30 kilometer
interconnector pipeline from the Summail field to the Dohuk power
plant, which was running on diesel/light fuel and is expected to fully
run on gas by the end of 2014. It is projected that the use of gas for the
Dohuk power plant will save about $100 million on expensive fuel
each month.[19]

Impact Assessment: Electricity Sector

The influx of refugees and IDPs has had an impact on the KRI electricity
sector. For example, the Erbil electricity network demand load reached
its peak in August 2014, which represents a 22 percent increase compared with August 2013. A similar trend is seen in Sulaymaniyah: The
maximum demand for electricity in 2014 recorded was 1,447 megawatts
in February 2014. Considering the increase in the number of people displaced to Sulaymaniyah in 2014, it is expected that the demand for electricity in the coming winter will be higher than the previous record,
which means that 125 megawatts of additional capacity would be needed.
In total, an additional 600 to 700 megawatts of generation capacity would
be needed to maintain the network balance in KRI.

The World Bank ESIA relied on the SEINA study and extended its
assumptions to assess the impact of the crisis over 2012–14. The previous
estimate of the financial cost of the electricity delivery was 13.34 cents per
kilowatt-hour. Under the assumption of increased efficiency of commissioned new state-of-the-art power plants, relatively well-implemented
transmission and distribution investments over the last two to three years,
and progressive introduction of cheaper natural gas as a substitute of
expensive fuels, the financial cost of the electricity delivery has been
downwardly revised to 12.9 cents, 9.3 cents, and 7.2 cents per kilowatt-
hour for 2012, 2013, and 2014, respectively. In addition, the World Bank
relied on Ministry of Electricity estimates of the costs of the required
investments and service delivery for electricity for refugees and IDPs living

FIGURE 3.1
Fiscal Cost of Electricity Delivery in KRI, 2010–15

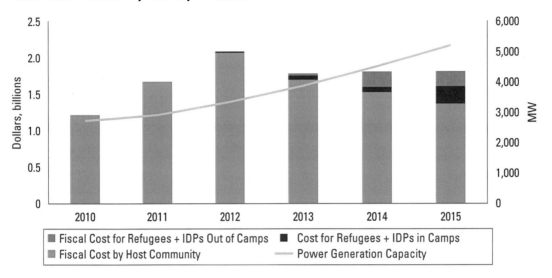

Note: IDPs = internally displaced persons.

in camps.[20] As a result, the impact assessment is evaluated at $383 million between the fourth quarter of 2012 and the end of 2014 (figure 3.1).

Stabilization Assessment: Electricity Sector

Additional resources are needed to provide electricity to the increased population in 2015. The World Bank estimates that about $275 million will be required to satisfy the needs of refugees and IDPs. Under the low scenario for population estimates, the stabilization cost is estimated at $364 million, whereas under the high scenario, the stabilization cost is estimated at $517 million. Table 3.4 presents the stabilization assessment for the electricity sector.

Transportation Sector

The combination of the ISIS crisis, influx of IDPs, and indirectly the Syrian refugees has caused an increase in the wear and tear of the road network and has damaged several bridges and road sections. The crisis has resulted in the closure of one of the main trade routes between north and south from Dohuk to Erbil via Mosul. IDPs who fled their homes using their own vehicles caused an abrupt increase in traffic by about 20 percent. The humanitarian relief efforts, including heavy supply

TABLE 3.4
Stabilization Assessment for the Electricity Sector, 2015 Projection
dollars, millions

	Baseline[a]		Low Scenario[b]		High Scenario[c]	
	Syrian Refugees	IDPs	Syrian Refugees	IDPs	Syrian Refugees	IDPs
Stabilization (needs) assessment	64.8	210.0	79.7	283.9	114.6	402.6
Current spending	60.2	188.1	68.9	210.1	89.2	276.7
Capital spending	4.6	21.9	10.8	73.9	25.4	125.9

Note: IDPs = internally displaced persons.
a. Status quo—the current population of Syrian refugees and IDPs remains unchanged.
b. Additional influx of 30,000 Syrian refugees and 250,000 Iraqi IDPs.
c. Additional influx of 100,000 Syrian refugees and 500,000 Iraqi IDPs.

trucks carrying food, medicine, and construction material (more so than the Syrian refugees themselves, who are mostly lower income and housed in shelters outside the major cities in Dohuk), have also added a toll on the road network. All these factors have contributed to the increase in congestion, travel time, traffic accidents, and wear and tear of the local road network. The crisis, primarily the fighting with ISIS, has also had severe impacts on parts of the network, especially at the Syrian frontier as well as Mosul Governorate. Eight bridges in the three governorates (Erbil, Dohuk, and Sulaymaniyah) have already been either fully or partially destroyed by the recent military conflict.

The crisis has also taken a toll on the municipal road network. The 20 percent increase in traffic together with minimal investment in road maintenance and lack of a public transport system have caused severe traffic congestion, especially in the main cities of Sulaymaniyah and Dohuk. Despite the needs, noticeable increases have not been seen in public expenditures in the transport sector linked to the Syrian crisis or IDPs.

Transportation in KRI before the Crisis

Asset preservation: Roads and bridges sector

The road network in KRI is in generally fair to poor condition. The road network is composed of primary, secondary, and tertiary (local/municipal/village) roads with a total KRI network of about 23,400 kilometers.

The main roads, however, comprise approximately 5,800 kilometers, out of which 1,954 kilometers are primary and 3,854 kilometers are secondary roads (table 3.5), and the remaining majority belongs to local roads. The primary and secondary road network is mostly paved, with only about 52 kilometers identified as earth, gravel, or tracks. However, tertiary roads are mostly unpaved (almost 13,920 kilometers). In total, nearly 60 percent of the roads are not paved. About 98 percent of the roads have one lane per direction, and the remaining 2 percent (482 kilometers) have two lanes or more on a dual carriageway. A significant proportion of the existing road network (15,480 kilometers or 66 percent) is in poor to critical (very poor) condition in terms of pavement condition, as measured by the Pavement Condition Index.[21] Most of this is made up of tertiary roads (14,670 kilometers). The primary and secondary network is mostly in good to fair condition, with 28 percent having poor to failed pavements.

The condition of bridges and other major structures is alarming. There are 328 bridges in KRI, 95 percent of which are in need of urgent maintenance work and/or rectification. The nonattendance of this need is likely to cost more in the future because of further exponential deterioration and have possible consequences in terms of injuries, fatalities, and damage to property.

Institutional capacity, including management of the road network, is gradually being developed. The General Directorate for Roads and Bridges under the Ministry of Housing and Construction has the overall mandate to plan, construct, and maintain the main roads network, and the road departments at the governorate and municipal levels oversee such roles for the local roads. Over the past few years, road asset management systems have been developed, and General

TABLE 3.5
Distribution of Road Network in KRG Governorates
kilometers

Governorate	Length, by Road Type			
	Primary	**Secondary**	**Tertiary**	**Total**
Erbil	699	1,398	6,038	8,135
Dohuk	542	1,010	3,528	5,080
Sulaymaniyah and Garmian	713	1,446	8,012	10,171
Total	**1,954**	**3,854**	**17,578**	**23,386**

Directorate for Roads and Bridges' staff have been trained for overall road management.

The political standoff with the central government in Baghdad together with the limited transfers of monthly allocations to KRG have contributed to a severe slowdown in implementing either new or ongoing construction and maintenance contracts. Such a drop in financing matched with an increase in traffic, especially by IDPs in 2014, has had an impact on the quality of the road network. Investments in road construction and maintenance have been impacted in 2014 with very few resources allocated. During 2010–13, KRG made substantial investments in improving its road network, allocating about $544 million to this sector in the three governorates. This investment includes about $316 million for new roads construction and $228 million for maintenance. KRG's investment in maintaining the main and secondary roads (5,800 kilometers) averaged about $57 million annually, but the needs are about $60 million (table 3.6).

Additional resources would be needed for road construction. Recent studies[22] of construction and maintenance projects in KRI showed that

PHOTO 3.2
Kawergosk Refugee Camp in Erbil Governorate

Thousands of families entered the Kurdistan Region of Iraq at the end of 2014 because of increased conflict in Kobani, Syria. This newly arrived family was provided with emergency relief as soon as they arrived to Kawergosk Refugee Camp, Erbil Governorate, October 2014. © UNHCR/T. Tool. Used with the permission of UNHCR/T. Tool; further permission required for reuse.

TABLE 3.6
Construction and Maintenance Expenditures in the Road Sector Excluding Municipal Road Network, 2010–13
dollars, millions

Category	2010	2011	2012	2013
Construction expenditures				
Erbil	5.50	22.10	6.80	1.50
Dohuk	21.06	12.49	6.60	13.19
Sulaymaniyah	88.70	39.40	42.20	56.30
Maintenance expenditures				
Erbil	13.03	8.11	16.07	28.15
Dohuk	9.89	7.36	13.24	13.75
Sulaymaniyah	16.30	12.80	51.60	38.00
Subtotal (construction expenditures)	115.26	73.99	55.6	70.99
Subtotal (maintenance expenditures)	39.22	28.27	80.91	79.90
Total	**154.48**	**102.26**	**136.51**	**150.89**

additional $230 million would be necessary for upgrade of 820 kilometers of major tertiary roads, that is, widening of gravel roads or unpaved to paved. The maintenance plan for primary and secondary roads for the same period showed that almost 85 percent of existing roads (approximately 4,860 kilometers) will require some kind of heavy maintenance, with some 25 percent of this within the first five years. The expected budget for maintenance of major roads has been estimated at $779 million (26.3 percent of which to be spent in Dohuk, 38.6 percent in Erbil, and 35 percent in Sulaymaniyah and Garmian), $216 million of which within the next five years. The total cost for construction of new road infrastructure in the next 20 years has been estimated at $10.6 billion (17.6 percent of which to be invested in Dohuk, 34.6 percent in Erbil, and 47.8 percent in Sulaymaniyah and Garmian), with almost 53 percent of this amount to be spent within the first five years. This involves a total of 3,359 kilometers of projects, including 2,407 kilometers of new roads, 926 kilometers of widened roads, 21 kilometers of new tunnels, and 5 kilometers of new bridges.

The municipal road network has also been impacted by the refugee and IDP influx. The municipal road network is also taking a toll and requires additional resources for not only maintenance, but also expansion to serve the inflow of displaced people. To meet KRG's development plans, municipalities have invested about $865 million in developing and maintaining their network over the last four years (table 3.7).

TABLE 3.7

Construction and Maintenance Expenditures in the Road Sector, Municipal Road Network, 2010–13

dollars, millions

Category	2010	2011	2012	2013
Construction expenditures				
Erbil	20.90	53.20	104.50	5.70
Dohuk	0.48	66.50	76.00	7.60
Sulaymaniyah	3.80	38.00	17.10	27.55
Maintenance expenditures				
Erbil	1.10	2.80	5.50	0.30
Dohuk	0.03	3.50	4.00	0.40
Sulaymaniyah	0.20	2.00	0.90	1.45
Subtotal (construction expenditures)	25.18	157.70	197.60	40.85
Subtotal (maintenance expenditures)	1.33	8.30	10.40	2.15
Total	**26.50**	**166.00**	**208.00**	**43.00**

Source: KRG Ministry of Municipalities and Tourism 2014.

The strategic road network is, in general, uncongested, even at peak periods. Most of the main road network is operating under an "A" level of service,[23] and less than 0.5 percent operates under a "D" level of service or worse. Generally no important seasonality effects can be detected on the network. Privately owned cars account for more than 40 percent of the traffic on roads, and vans, pickups, and light goods vehicles account for about 25 percent, followed by heavy goods vehicles for about 17 percent. Average vehicle occupancy rates are relatively high in the region, with 2.2 passengers per car, 2.9 passengers per taxi, 2 passengers per van pickup/light goods vehicle, and 1.4 passengers per heavy goods vehicle, on average.

Traffic demand and accident rates have one of the greatest growth rates in the area. On the basis of the past few years' data, a trend of annual traffic demand growth for 2010–30 should be ranging between 3.1 and 6.3 percent[24] depending on the type of demand (freight, car, or public transport) and regional employment level. The level of injuries and fatalities caused by traffic accidents is a growing social and economic cost for the region. There were 678 reported deaths from road accidents in KRI in 2011. A rapid increase in deaths began in 2006: 641 compared with 389 in 2005, and fewer in earlier years. Road accident rates seem to be growing at an alarming rate, in particular in Dohuk (injury growth of 64 percent each year between

2006 and 2009) and Erbil (injury growth of 141 percent each year between 2006 and 2009).

Asset preservation: Public transport sector

The extent and capacity of the public transport system in KRI is dominated by the usage of taxis. No mass transit is present in KRI cities, be it a regular intercity railway, light rail transit, or bus rapid transit. However, the Ministry of Transportation and Communications, responsible for the public transport sector in KRI, is planning to organize the bus system and introduce mass transit systems in Erbil and Sulaymaniyah. The number of passenger buses in KRI in 2010 was 5,082 buses, of which 3,490 were intracity buses and 1,592 were intercity buses. The number of taxis was 55,331, of which 52,500 were intracity taxis and 2,831 were intercity taxis. The total number of passengers using these services was 5.13 million in 2010, the majority of whom (about 75 percent) were passengers of intracity taxis.

Asset preservation: Railways sector

Currently KRI does not have an operational railway. Iraq has a railway network of about 2,100 kilometers extending from Basrah in the south through Baghdad to Qaem and the Syrian border to the west, and to Kirkuk, Mosul, and Rabiah at the Syrian border to the north. However, KRI has yet to link to the network. The recently completed railway master plan presents a clear vision for the development of the network including linkages between Kirkuk, Erbil, Mosul, and Dohuk to the Turkish border. The plan also intends to connect Jordan and the Islamic Republic of Iran.

Asset preservation: Airports sector

Two international airports are operational in Erbil and Sulaymaniyah. A third airport in Dohuk is currently under construction. Although the existing airports seem to be meeting demands, air cargo facilities may require further expansion (UN-HABITAT 2012), which could further strengthen the region's logistics potential. A weak link is regional air cargo capability, however. Neither of the existing airports has adequate air cargo facilities, and bureaucratic procedures for cargo imports and exports are heavily criticized by users. A move toward electronic data interchange for cargo movements and customs formalities is overdue. The lack of a cold chain for fruit, vegetables, flowers, or other potential exports is also a handicap.

Freight and Transit Activities

Freight services are provided by a trucking sector that is highly fragmented and with a generally outdated fleet. There are about 345 transportation companies for goods and 44 companies to transport oil products, most of which are based in Erbil. Most trucking companies own only one truck, although a few small fleets are operated.

Iraq's trade is primarily with Turkey with significant goods transported across the main border crossing at Ibrahim Al-Khalil. However, several other borders crossings are found with the Islamic Republic of Iran. The main cross-border locations in the north are the following: Ibrahim Al-Khalil-Khabur (Turkey), Parwiz Khan-Qasr Shiren (the Islamic Republic of Iran), Halabja-Nowsud (the Islamic Republic of Iran), Bashmagh-Mariwan (the Islamic Republic of Iran), Mawat-Bana (the Islamic Republic of Iran), Phishdar-Sardasht (the Islamic Republic of Iran), and Haji Omran-Piran Shahr (the Islamic Republic of Iran). About 50 percent of Iraq's imports come through its north–south corridor and enter through the Ibrahim Al-Khalil border crossing from the European Union, Russia, and Central Asia via Turkey. In 2013, about 3,000 heavy trucks entered Iraq daily from Turkey through the Ibrahim Al-Khalil border crossing. In recent months this figure has dropped to fewer than 700 a day.

Impact of the Crisis on the Transport Sector and Stabilization Needs

The Syrian and IDP crises led to an increase in transport costs. The closing of the Bajen refinery in Mosul, the main supplier of bitumen and fuel to KRI governorates, together with the closure of the main road corridor from Dohuk to Erbil via Mosul, have led to an increase in the price of bitumen from $400 to $620 per ton and $500 to $600 per ton in Dohuk and Erbil, respectively, as well as to an increase in fuel prices. The latter has caused an increase in transport cost by 50 percent. Vehicle operating costs have increased because of diversion of traffic to lesser capacity and dirt roads.

The combination of the budget crisis and influx of IDPs and refugees may have caused an increase in wear and tear on the road network. The crises have resulted in the closure of one of the main trade routes between north and south from Dohuk to Erbil via Mosul, IDPs who fled their homes using their own vehicles caused an abrupt increase in traffic by about 20 percent, and the humanitarian relief efforts may have added a toll on the road network. The impact on the road network could have been more severe should the trade volume between Iraq and Turkey continue at the same levels of precrisis.

The ISIS crisis has also had severe impacts on parts of the network, especially that at the frontier with Syrian borders as well as Mosul governorate. Eight bridges in the three governorates (Erbil, Dohuk, and Sulaymaniyah) have already been either fully or partially destroyed by recent military conflict. In addition, important road segments have also been destroyed or blocked. Therefore new alternate road links, including bridges, will need to be constructed in the near future to provide important links between the governorates and major cities. In addition, pavement of dirt roads leading to refugee camps will also be necessary.

Preserving the road network (outside municipalities) to similar precrisis conditions would require an additional spending on maintenance of $15.4 million and $20.3 million under the low (25 percent traffic increase) and high (30 percent traffic increase) scenarios, respectively, in 2015.[25] Most of the wear and tear will occur in governorates with a high refugee influx, such as Dohuk and Sulaymaniyah.

Restoring the municipal road network to similar precrisis conditions would also require an additional $5.2 million and $6.1 million under the low (35 percent traffic increase) and high (40 percent traffic increase) scenarios, respectively, in 2015.[25] These figures are based on the low case scenario, which is equivalent to 30 percent and 35 percent increase in municipal traffic for 2014 and 2015, respectively.

Therefore, the sum of additional funding required for maintenance of main roads and municipal road networks would be $20.6 million for the low case scenario and $26.4 million for the high case scenario. This will be needed for the reconstruction of roads and bridges damaged in the Syrian and ISIS conflicts and new access to refugee camps. Initial estimates from the roads directorates in Erbil and Dohuk show the need for about $26.5 million to repair the damage caused directly by the conflict, whether through bombing essential roads and bridges between Dohuk, Mosul, and Erbil or through the toll on diverting all traffic, including heavy traffic, on roads with much smaller capacities. Of this amount, $7.5 million would be allocated to repair the damaged bridges and rehabilitate and maintain about 120 kilometers of roads. Moreover, an additional $19 million will be needed to construct 50 kilometers of road access to the refugee camps.

Notes

1. In the range of $1 per month for an apartment in Erbil and Dohuk.
2. Data from the Ministry of Water, SEINA report, and World Bank staff calculations.

3. The use of wells is estimated at 35 percent in Erbil City center and 40 percent outside the city. In Sulaymaniyah, in the city it is 2 percent but it reaches 70 percent outside the city; and in Dohuk it is 2 percent in the city and 40 percent outside the city.

4. Data provided by the Ministry of Municipalities and Tourism.

5. Based on http://reliefweb.int/sites/reliefweb.int/files/resources/Revision_2014 _Iraq_SRP.pdf the cost of providing water and sanitation is about $40 per person per month.

6. Estimation by Ministry of Municipalities General Directorates of Municipalities in Dohuk and Erbil.

7. Out-of-camp refugees and IDPs assumed to generate the same amount of per capita daily solid waste as the host communities.

8. Per capita solid waste generated only, not counting industrial, commercial, military, and hospital solid waste. A media source estimated recently that this amount is equal to the total solid waste generated in KRI by the population (Alexander Whitcomb, RUDAW Media Network, September 5, 2014, http://rudaw.net/english/about).

9. Based on information from the Ministry of Municipalities and Tourism, Directorate General of Duhok Municipalities, September 2014.

10. http://www.citypopulation.de/Iraq.html, 2011.

11. At the time of writing the report, estimations were available for Erbil Governorate, Dohuk Governorate, and Sulaymaniyah City (excluding the rest of Sulaymaniyah Governorate).

12. All-weather cabinets will be installed to replace camps for IDPs and refugees for extended temporary stays in KRI.

13. Based on average baseline period (2011) and estimates received for governorates of Dohuk and Erbil and Sulaymaniyah City.

14. Average calculated by the World Bank team on the basis of Sulaymaniyah Governorate with 71 percent of daily waste being organic, and Erbil City with 56 percent of solid waste generated being organic. Information from the Ministry of Municipalities and Tourism, Presidency of Erbil Municipality, Directorate for Municipality Services and Environment.

15. Estimates for 2014 (without refugees and IDPs) provided by the Ministry of Municipalities and Tourism, Presidency of Erbil Municipality, Directorate of Services and Environment Municipality.

16. Reported by the Ministry of Municipalities and Tourism, Presidency of Erbil Municipality, Directorate of Services and Environment Municipality. It is likely that the number is slightly higher because of higher amounts of solid waste per capita generated in Erbil's four main IDPs camps.

17. Estimated as 80 percent by the Sulaymaniyah Municipality.

18. In 2013, the KRG Ministry of Finance provided ID 80 billion support to the sector each month ($770 million for 2013).

19. KRG Ministry of Natural Resources, Press Release, May 26, 2014.

20. These estimates are as follows: There are five individuals living in each tent; the cost of the electricity distribution networks is $2,100 per tent; the cost of constructing the electricity transmission networks is $500 per tent; the cost of access to electricity is $305 per tent per year; and the cost of fuel to cover energy needs is $1,433 per tent per year.

21. From the pavement condition surveys for the KRG Road Asset Management Study (2013).

22. KRG Road Asset Management (2013) and Highway Master Plan (2012b).

23. "A" is free-flow condition and "F" is forced or breakdown flow.

24. KRG Highway Master Plan (2012b).

25. Based on World Bank calculations.

KRG Impact Assessment, 2012–14

TABLE A.1
KRG Impact Assessment, 2012–14
dollars, millions

	2012	2013	2014	
			Syrian Refugee and Iraqi IDP Influx	
	Syrian Refugee Influx	Syrian Refugee Influx	Syrian Refugee Influx	Iraqi IDP Influx
Human Development				
Health	**1.3**	**19.7**	**5.5**	**19.7**
Current spending	1.3	19.7	5.5	19.7
Primary health care	0.3	3.9	1.1	3.9
Hospital	1.1	15.7	4.4	15.8
Education		**0.6**	**3.1**	
Capital spending		0.6	3.1	
School construction/rehabilitation		0.6	3.1	
Food Security	**2.1**	**9.0**	**4.1**	**14.6**
Current spending				
Food security	2.1	9.0	4.1	14.6
Total: Human Development	**3.4**	**29.3**	**47.1**	
Infrastructure				
Energy	**9.2**	**35.5**	**70.0**	**250.0**
Current spending	9.2	35.5	67.8	242.1
Additional fuel cost	2.1	11.9	25.5	91.0
Financial subsidy to electricity sector	7.1	23.6	42.3	151.0
Capital spending			2.2	7.9
Cost of electricity infrastructure in camps			2.2	7.9
Solid Waste Management	**0.3**	**0.5**	**0.6**	**1.0**
Current spending	0.2	0.3	0.4	0.6
Capital spending	0.1	0.2	0.2	0.4
Water	**4.3**	**2.6**	**6.4**	**19.7**
Current spending	4.3	2.6	2.3	7.1
Capital spending	0.0	0.0	4.1	12.6
Memo: Humanitarian (UNICEF, UNHCR, etc.)	19.7	48.7	52.5	78.8
Total: Infrastructure	**13.7**	**38.5**	**77.0**	**270.6**
Grand Total: Human Development and Infrastructure	**17.2**	**67.8**	**394.7**	

Note: IDP = internally displaced person.

Methodology: KRG Economic and Social Impact Assessment

Impact Assessment

For each variable of interest, the assessment of the impact of the conflict is measured through the following methodology: the difference between (1) the actual outturn (spending) for that variable in period t and (2) the spending that would have occurred in period t should the conflict had not occurred (counterfactual).

The exact approach to estimate the counterfactual spending is guided by data availability. Possible approaches include (1) using the current and capital budget data actuals, (2) using KRG's Vision 2020, or (3) extrapolating from preconflict trends. In all these approaches, special care is exercised to incorporate known exogenous factors that would impact the counterfactual forecast, for example, if a policy change that is not related to the conflict were introduced, this is eliminated from the data used to build the counterfactual.

Because quantitative data are limited at the regional level, the aforementioned quantitative methodology is complemented by a more qualitative approach that looks at the social impact and institutional implications of the crisis.

To estimate the social impact and institutional implications, secondary literature assessments are carried out bringing together the data from government sources, as well as assessments carried out by the UN and multilateral, bilateral, and nongovernmental organizations (NGOs).

Stabilization Needs Assessment

For each variable of interest, the assessment of the stabilization needs generated by the conflict is measured by the difference between (1) the spending that would have been needed in period t to maintain the preconflict level of quality and access to public services for the host communities and refugees and IDPs and (2) the spending that would have occurred in period t should the conflict had not occurred (counterfactual).

Several approaches are possible to estimate the spending that would have been needed to maintain quality and access of public services to a preconflict level. The simplest would be to use average unit cost estimate (separately for current and capital spending). The quality and access indicators used have an important bearing on the estimate obtained, so these are chosen very carefully. These indicators would likely be the key performance indicators that each ministry might have; if these are not available, external indicators are used.

The social impact and institutional implications take into account community and local perspectives and assess, to the extent possible, current capacities at the municipal and community level to deal with the crisis and enhance their resilience.

The aforementioned quantitative and qualitative stabilization assessment will result in a prioritized and sequenced plan in which the priority results are those that will help the stabilization of KRG.

Simulation Model: Fiscal Impact of the Conflict

FIGURE C.1
Simulation Model: Impact of the Conflict

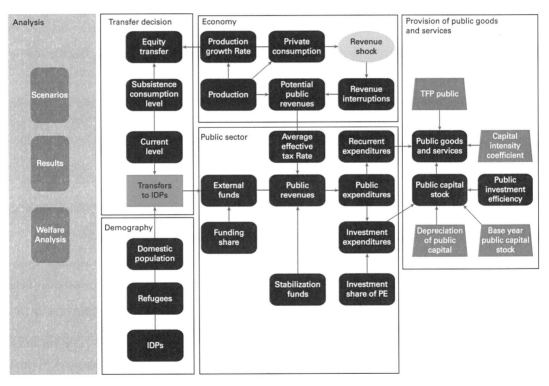

Note: IDPs = internally displaced persons; PE = public expenditure; TFP = total factor productivity.

Modeling the Macroeconomic Impact of IDPs

In this technical appendix, the modeling framework built for simulating the macroeconomic impact of IDPs and refugees is discussed. The economic environment comprises an exogenous income-generating process, public sector provision of goods and services, and demographic characteristics of the native and IDP populations. Appendix C shows the outline of the interactions among these aspects visually.

Characterizing the Economic Environment

Demography

The native population of KRI is denoted by N_t in year t, where the natural rate of population growth is given by n_t. Therefore, $N_t = N_{t-1} \times (1 + n_t)$.

The size of IDPs and refugees in year t, on the other hand, is given by P_t. Changes in this number are assumed to be driven exogenously, and they are not correlated with the value in the previous year. Thus, $P_t = P_{t-1} + \Delta P$. Overall, therefore, $M_t = N_t + P_t$ people are in the region in year t.

Economy

On the basis of discussions with KRG authorities, for the purposes of this analysis, we assume that the potential output of the KRI economy is in the form of endowments, which grows at an exogenous rate g_t, so that

$$Y_t = Y_{t-1} \times (1 + g_t),$$

where Y_t denotes the exogenous income in year t. The growth rate consists of a trend growth rate and idiosyncratic shock. Formally,

$$g_t = \bar{g} + \epsilon_t, \ \epsilon \sim N(0, \sigma^\epsilon).$$

The value of the 2014 growth shock is predetermined, which captures the effects of recent surge in conflict and canceled public projects as a result of interruptions in oil revenue transfers from Baghdad. Overall, however, the exogenous character of the growth process is preserved to a large extent because hydrocarbon production was not affected by these factors.

Public Sector

KRG captures a portion of the exogenous income in the form of tax and nontax revenues from the private sector and receives transfers from the Baghdad government. Total public revenues can, then, be characterized as a share of exogenous income:

$$R_t = t_t \times Y_t,$$

where R_t is the public revenues at time t, and t_t is the revenue share of the public sector. To reflect the uncertainty in central government transfers, we assume that this share is also a stochastic process:

$$t_t = \bar{t} + \mu_t, \mu \sim N(0, \ \sigma^\mu)$$

The shock to revenues in 2014 is imposed arbitrarily to reflect the size of unexpected disruptions in central government transfers. The budget constraint of the KRG is given by the following:

$$R_t + B_t = \tau_t P_t + G_t + \gamma B_{t-1},$$

where B_t denotes the public sector debt issuance, τ_t. is the per capita transfer to IDPs, and G_t is the other public expenditures that eventually are used for providing public goods and services to the people of KRI. In the absence of reliable data for debt issuances, we assume that $B_t = \gamma = 0$.

Provision of public goods and services is denoted by the following technology:

$$\Phi_t = A_t K_t^\alpha L_t^{1-\alpha},$$

where L_t is the employment in provision of public goods and services, and K_t is the public capital stock, which exhibits the following law of motion:

$$K_t = (1 - \delta)K_{t-1} + \beta\lambda G_t,$$

where δ is the rate of depreciation in capital stock, λ is the share of public expenditures that is allocated to public investments (therefore, $(1 - \lambda)$ percent of them are allocated for recurrent expenditures), and β is a parameter that shows the public investment efficiency, $0 < \delta, \lambda, \beta < 1$. Overall, public capital stock in year t is equal to the last year's capital stock net of depreciation and net effective investments in year t.

Overall, the budgetary shock in 2014 leads to a reduction in provision of public goods and services as a result of reductions in public investments and recurrent expenditures. Similarly, a surge in IDP inflow also affects the public finances by reducing the money allocated to provision of public goods and services.

Assessment of Impact

The presence of IDPs affects the welfare of the native population in two channels:

- First, the overall provision of public goods and services diminishes because a portion of public funds is diverted to finance the transfers to IDPs and

- Second, the native population's access to public goods and services is constrained because of congestion, for example, an increase in the number of beneficiaries.

The first effect is "direct" and can be measured in a relatively straightforward way. The second observation is based on the following rationale. Most public goods and services are "public goods" when atomistic decision making is considered; for example, they are nonrival and nonexcludable at the microlevel. For example, the birth of one more citizen does not require additional military expenditures to keep public security at the original level. However, a 20 percent increase in total population makes these goods and services rival one another as a result of congestion. For example, access to public hospitals could significantly deteriorate if the IDP population in a city is relatively large in comparison to the native population. These "indirect" effects are typically not captured in standard macroeconomic impact analyses.

To capture both direct and indirect effects, we define a "Monetary Well-Being" function for the native individuals. Formally:

$$u^i = \frac{1}{N_t}(1 - t_t) \cdot Y_t + \frac{1}{N_t + P_t} \cdot \Phi_t.$$

The first term on the right-hand side of the above equation denotes the private disposable income available to each native KRI resident, and the second term shows the per person access to public goods and services regardless of origin (IDP or native). This formulation reflects the fact that we did not consider the effects of IDPs on private consumption, mainly because the IDP demand for private goods is thought to have no impact on domestic prices because most consumption goods are imported.

In the absence of the presence of IDPs, the monetary well-being would be the following:

$$u^{i'} = \frac{1}{N_t}(1 - t_t) \cdot Y_t + \frac{1}{N_t} \cdot \Phi'_t.$$

The total impact of IDPs on the monetary well-being of native KRI residents is given by

$$\sum_{i=1}^{N_t} (u^i - u^{i'}) = N_t \cdot \left[\frac{\Phi_t}{N_t + P_t} - \frac{\Phi'_t}{N_t} \right].$$

Note that this approach provides a measure of contemporaneous impact, for example, a point in time difference in monetary well-beings, which is a flow variable. A dynamic impact analysis would compare the monetary well-being in two different income and public goods and services provision trajectories going forward. Then the present values of these two paths would be compared to calculate the impacts in dynamic form. In KRI, however, such an analysis is not possible because of the very limited availability of data and projections.

Dohuk Governorate: Internally Displaced Persons

MAP E.1
Dohuk Governorate: Internally Displaced Persons

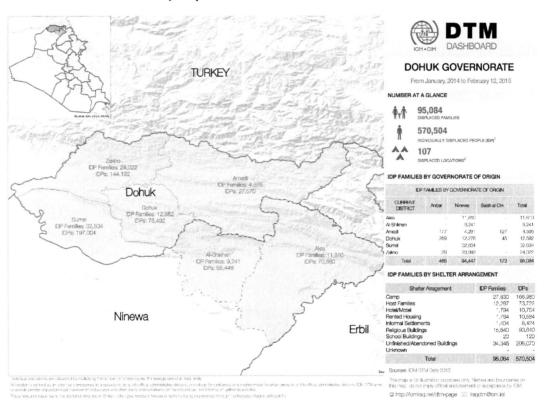

© International Organization for Migration. Used with the permission of the International Organization for Migration; further permission required for reuse.
Note: IDPs = internally displaced persons.

Erbil Governorate: Internally Displaced Persons

MAP F.1
Erbil Governorate: Internally Displaced Persons

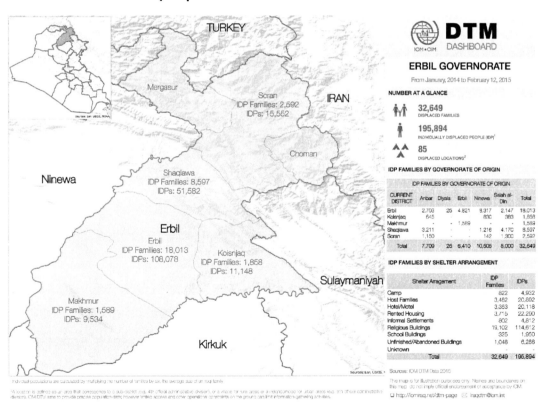

© International Organization for Migration. Used with the permission of the International Organization for Migration; further permission required for reuse.

Note: IDPs = internally displaced persons.

APPENDIX G

Sulaymaniyah Governorate: Internally Displaced Persons

MAP G.1

Sulaymaniyah Governorate: Internally Displaced Persons

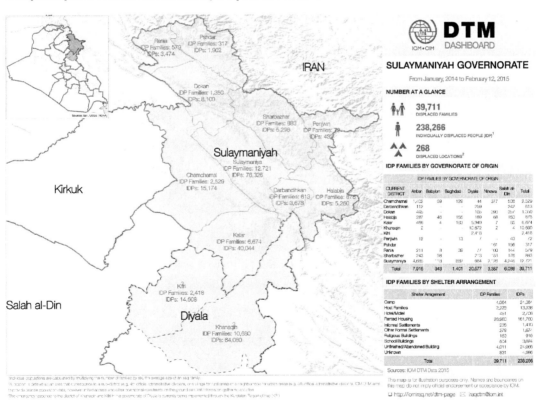

© International Organization for Migration. Used with the permission of the International Organization for Migration; further permission required for reuse.

Note: IDPs = internally displaced persons.

Estimates of the Economic
Impact of the ISIS Crisis
Attributable to Trade

Transport costs in KRI have increased because of the increase in fuel costs and may also have been affected by changes in trade volumes and trade balance. The reduction in KRI's role as a route for transit trade between Turkey and Iraq, and between the Islamic Republic of Iran and Iraq, is likely to have also had an adverse effect on KRI's transport costs. Using the 2011 Turkish input-output table from the World Input Output Tables, it is estimated that the transport sector accounts for 8–12 percent of GDP, depending on the definition of the sector.[1] We assume that transport in KRI represents 10 percent of the cost of traded goods (preshock). A 50 percent increase in transport prices implies that the transport sector now represents about 12 percent of the cost of goods postshock. This is assumed exogenous to KRI, so the shock acts like a 2 percentage point increase in world prices for imports and a 2 percentage point decrease for world prices for exports.

According to mirror data from COMTRADE, in 2013, the value of Iraq's merchandise imports was $38 billion and merchandise exports were $88 billion. According to International Monetary Fund estimates, KRI represents roughly 10 percent of Iraqi GDP (International Monetary Fund 2013). We could use this fact to impute to KRI about 10 percent of all trade activity measured at the level of Iraq. We would then estimate Kurdistan regional imports to be $3.8 billion and its exports to be $8.8 billion. But the independent import data provided by the KRG Ministry of Trade and Industry indicate that KRI's imports were about one-third of overall Iraqi exports and valued at about $20.8 billion in 2013. Acknowledging this is a rough estimate, we apply this to Iraqi trade statistics. More could possibly be done to pin down a better estimate of the

FIGURE H.1
Import Demand and Export Supply

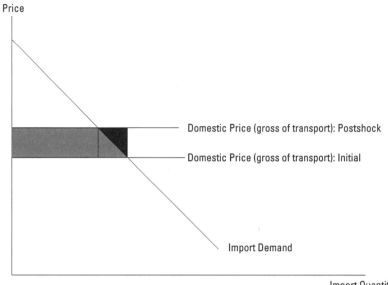

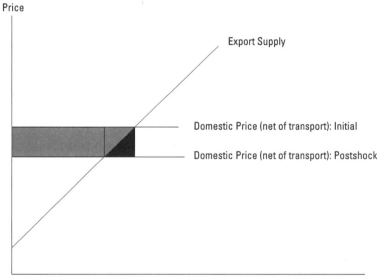

Kurdish share on the export side, given that we know exports are almost all oil.

In a simple import demand or export supply framework the 2 percentage point ad valorem change in world prices has an impact on welfare according to the following formula:

$$\Delta W = value\ of\ trade\ [\Delta t - 0.5(\Delta t)^2\varepsilon,], \tag{1}$$

where

ΔW is the change in welfare associated with a given trade flow

Δt (=0.02) is the percentage point change in the transport cost share of total cost and

ε is an estimate of the relevant trade elasticity.

On the basis of estimates in the literature, we choose an elasticity of five. This value is not important for these calculations (as it would be for studies of tariff changes, which affect government revenues). However, note that an elasticity of five would suggest that a 2 percent increase in international prices (resulting from a 20 percent increase in trade costs) leads to a 10 percent change in trade. We have observed reductions in imports of about 45 percent and argued that between one-quarter and one-third is attributable to the budget freeze. The remaining 10 to 120 percent change in imports is broadly consistent with the estimates we use here.

The first term in brackets in equation (1) is the rectangle (increased costs of serving the initial imports and exports). The second term is the triangle that complements the Harberger triangle: It is the cost that does not have to be paid because imports and exports are lower.

The welfare multiplier of trade value is [0.02−0.001] = 0.019.

Losses from more expensive imports = 0.019×$20.785 billion = $394 million (2013 dollars). (The import value of $3.8 billion would produce a loss estimate of $72 million.)

Losses from lower prices for exports = 0.019×8.8 billion = $167.2 million (2013 dollars).

Total trade losses (annualized) = $561 million (compared with 239.4 million if imports were only $3.8 billion).

Total trade losses (per month) = $561 million/12 = $46.75 million per month (compared with 20 million per month with the lower import figure).

Trade-related losses as a share of GRP (assume GRP of $20 billion) = 0.561/20 = 0.028, or 2.8 percent of GRP (compared with 1.2 of GRP with the lower import figure).

Per capita loss = 561/5 = $112 per citizen (assuming a population of 5 million).

Total impact on current citizens = $561 million.

Assuming impact per head on refugees and IDPs is the same as that on current citizens because of the increase in trade costs, total impact on 1 million refugees/IDPs = $112 million.

Therefore, total stabilization needs = $673 million.

The stabilization interventions could take the form of offsetting steps— for example, customs reform or road improvements—which reduce trade costs. It is worth emphasizing that these crude estimates do not include the impact on services trade and overall foreign investment.

There may be another reason why these figures may be underestimates. Analysis of the U.S. input-output table has revealed truck transport to be a general purpose technology (meaning that it serves as a reasonably important input into many if not all other sectors in the economy).[2]

The lesson of this discussion is that shocks to the productivity of general purpose technologies have much larger and much more enduring impacts on output than shocks to sectors that are not general purpose sectors (in the closed economy setting studied by these authors). The implications for open economies have not yet been studied, but presumably the lesson that shocks to the transport sector will have important spillover effects to the other sectors is an important consideration here.

Notes

1. Data are available from http://www.wiod.org/new_site/database/niots.htm.
2. Based on working paper, http://repositori.upf.edu/bitstream/handle/10230/6053/1206.pdf?sequence=1, with substantial changes. Facts about the truck transport sector are only in the working paper version.

Iraq and KRI Microfinance Sector Assessment

This technical appendix analyzes the impact of the ISIS conflict and Syrian refugee and IDP crisis on the sustainability of the Iraq microfinance sector, with specific reference to MFIs operating in KRI. The microfinance sector in Iraq has developed through nongovernmental organizations providing microcredit to informal micro- and small businesses and households. MFIs in Iraq have emerged as credible sources of financing for low-income households and entrepreneurs, both underserved by conventional banks. Microfinance in Iraq is generally used to promote household welfare by spurring economic activity and helping manage economic shocks (for example, unemployment, death in the family). Data presented were produced through stakeholder interviews and follow-up engagement with MFIs and industry support institutions, including the Iraq Microfinance Network and the MENA regional microfinance association (Sanabel). Meetings were also held with industry support institutions, including donors and technical assistance providers (for example, the SEEP network and the Consultative Group to Assist the Poor).

Snapshot: Microfinance in Iraq and KRI

History and Sectoral Outreach in Run-Up to ISIS Crisis

The microfinance sector in Iraq has grown significantly over the past 10 years, in large part because of extensive support from donors (most notably USAID) in funding and scaling-up of NGO MFIs. All of the MFIs in Iraq are NGOs. The microfinance sector in Iraq includes 12 NGO MFIs operating in all 18 provinces (figure I.1), with an outstanding portfolio totaling $150 million (ID 174.6 billion), equivalent to 0.25 percent of the

FIGURE I.1
Microfinance Industry Outreach

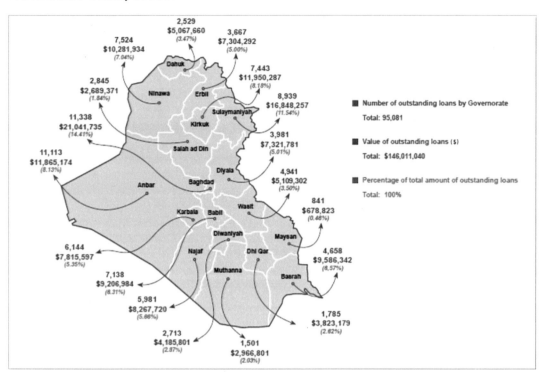

State of Iraq's microfinance industry, USAID Tijara, October 2012. © USAID. Used with the permission of USAID; further permission required for reuse.

banking sector's assets. The outstanding portfolio balance grew 17 percent in 2012, down from 48 percent in 2009. In addition to NGO MFIs, the Ministry of Labor and Social Affairs began microfinance programs in 2007, although the programs have used subsidized interest rates. With regard to penetration as a percentage of the overall population, the Iraq microfinance sector remains one of the smallest and least developed in the MENA region. The sector's growth is a product of the relatively high average loan size ($1,500) as opposed to client outreach levels. The industry's viability and growth continues to be challenged by civil conflict, with violence intensifying over the last year, and growing significantly in June 2014.

Two larger MFIs control more than half the market in Iraq: 38 percent of the outstanding portfolio is held by CHF, and 18 percent held by Al Thiqa. Ten other smaller MFIs thus hold the remaining 44 percent of the outstanding portfolio. MFIs currently do not offer savings, insurance, or payments and transfer services. Generally Iraqi MFIs can be divided in two categories: the large and fastest-growing MFIs, showing strong portfolio quality and profitability, and the smaller MFIs, witnessing much lower

TABLE I.1
Microfinance Providers as of 2012

Institution	Portfolio (dollars, millions)	%	Cumulative (%)	Active Clients	%	Cumulative (%)
CHF (operating in KRI)	45.0	30	30	20,414	21	21
Amalkom	5.0	3	33	7,868	8	29
Al Thiqa (operating in KRI)	34.0	23	56	15,572	16	44
Al Takadum[a]	12.0	8	64	12,023	12	57
Relief International (operating in KRI)	10.5	7	71	9,225	9	66
Izdiharuna (operating in KRI)	10.1	7	84	8,998	9	81
Al Bashaer	8.7	6	77	5,832	6	72
Al Aman	6.8	5	88	4,840	5	86
Bright Future Foundation (BFF) (based in and focus is in KRI)	6.7	4	93	4,527	5	90
Tallafar Economic Development Center (TEDC)[a]	6.1	4	97	5,310	5	96
Al Mosaned[a]	2.8	2	99	2,792	3	99
Al Tadhamun[a]	2.0	1	100	1,365	1	100
Total	**150.0**	**100**		**98,766**	**100**	

Source: Iraq Microfinance Network (IMFN), December 2012.
a. Operations now suspended because of the conflict.

growth rates and poorer portfolio quality. Before the recent escalation of violence due to ISIS and associated economic and social instability, outreach in Erbil, Sulaymaniyah, and Dohuk governorates was estimated to be approximately 15,198 loans outstanding valued at $29 million, representing 20 percent of the overall market share (based on percentage share of outstanding loans). One MFI, Bright Futures Foundation, is focused specifically on KRI, and various larger MFIs have operations in KRI governorates: CHF, Al Thiqa, Izdiharuna, Relief International, and Al Aman.

Demand for microfinance services has increased in this crisis period given the general environment of declining economic activity and investor uncertainty. The need for microcredit is particularly acute to manage household financial needs in this uncertain context, including managing risks (for example, responding to health emergencies), making productive investments (for example, education and home improvements), and developing income-generating activities and financing informal home-based businesses. Liquidity shortages in the banking sector, which were triggered by increased deposit withdrawal requests, have further increased the demand for microfinance.

Legal and Regulatory Framework Underpinning Microfinance Sector in Iraq and KRI

The microfinance sector is regulated by multiple laws and supervisors, each spanning varying degrees of control over the sector. NGO MFIs are regulated by the NGO directorate under the NGO law of 2010, which requires both national and international NGOs to register and conform to rules and requirements. There is a separate NGO law approved by the KRI parliament in 2011. Although NGO MFIs are registered under the NGO law, the Central Bank of Iraq (CBI) arguably has the right to regulate them as financial institutions. MFIs operating in KRI need to be registered with authorities both in Baghdad and in Erbil to be granted licenses and to operate legally.

Connected to the microfinance sector, numerous laws are aimed at supporting small business in Iraq that impact microfinance development. In 2012 the parliament passed the Support of Small Income-Generating Project Law, which provided a vehicle for the government to provide interest-free loans as well as tax exemptions to small businesses (no more than 10 employees). Similarly the small- and medium-sized enterprise (SME) finance company ordinance of 2010 explicitly allows commercial companies (SME Finance Companies) to engage in lending activities for SMEs, which can include microenterprises. SME finance companies are not permitted to engage in taking deposits. Despite this ordinance, no companies to date have been created. It is not clear whether this is because of regulatory barriers, obstacles to NGO MFI transformation, or business viability issues.

Impact of ISIS Conflict and Refugee Crisis on Iraq and KRI Microfinance Sector

Introduction and Snapshot of Key Issues

The ISIS conflict, refugee and IDP crisis, and associated economic shocks present both opportunities and risks for microfinance in KRI. In general, MFIs are reporting that demand for microfinance services has increased because of ongoing economic uncertainty, with clients look-ing to institutions as critical sources of financing to manage expendi-tures and invest in income-generating activities. This has been reinforced because of the liquidity issues and general weakness in the banking sector associated with the budget crisis. The crisis, however, has exacerbated operational weaknesses of MFIs as well as exposed regulatory and legal deficiencies in the sector. MFIs are reporting increased cases of nonrepayment by clients and corruption and deser-tion by MFI staff. These deficiencies are compounded by the fact that governance and transparency remain weak at many MFIs across Iraq. For example, many MFI boards are not functioning well and not effec-tively carrying out their oversight roles, and opportunities for training key staff are limited. The result has been the deterioration of opera-tional practices of MFIs, resulting in an increase in portfolio at risk and a slowdown of lending activity.

Similarly, accessible sources for institutional funding to grow credit portfolios—a critical issue before the current crisis—are now nonexistent. Many MFIs report being unable to access financing for operational expan-sion and, as a result, are not lending despite the general high demand for microfinance services. MFIs are unable to access certain bank branches and client segments because of security and in ISIS-controlled territories. Overall, these factors have forced a slowdown in lending activity. Four MFIs that were operating in conflict zones had to cease operations (Anbar, Tikrit, Mosul, Tel Afar). Although Iraq's microfinance industry was born in and has weathered significant insecurity, it seems doubtful that it can grow and thrive in an environment characterized by continued high levels of violence.

Negative Impacts of Crisis on the Iraqi and KRI Microfinance Sector

Four microfinance institutions (Tallafar, Al Mosamed, Al Tadhamum, Al Takadum) have stopped operations all together over the past six months because of the ongoing conflict and instability. These MFIs were operating in Anbar, Nineveh (Mosul, Tel Afar), and Salah ad Din gover-norates. The shutdown of these MFIs has impacted an estimated 21,490 active clients with $22 million in credit outstanding (figure I.2) and rep-resents an estimated 42,980 lost job opportunities. Approximately 15 percent of the overall microfinance market has been eliminated through the closing of these four institutions. This shutdown has occurred because of MFIs being unable to operate and access clients and branches because of ongoing violence and strict Sharia regulations imposed

FIGURE I.2
ISIS Conflict and Associated Instability Impact on Lending Activity in Iraq's Microfinance Sector, 2010–14

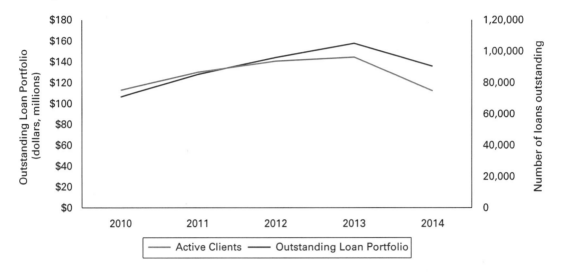

in ISIS-controlled territory. Risk of violence to staff is a significant threat, with one MFI reporting that ISIS kidnapped its executive director.

Portfolio at risk (PAR) greater than 30 days has increased substantially since the beginning of the crisis and is jeopardizing the ability of MFIs to continue operating (figure I.3). This has increased fivefold since its low of 0.7 percent in 2010 and has grown rapidly from 2012 to 2013, increasing from 1.3 percent at the end of June 2012, according to USAID Tijara figures,[1] to 3.5 percent at the end of October 2013, according to figures provided by the Iraq Microfinance Network. PAR now stands at an estimated 10 percent for many MFIs, with this figure being significantly higher for smaller MFIs (for example, 21 percent for Al-Bashaer and 35 percent in problem branches in KRI for Relief International).[2] Because of increases in nonrepayment, many smaller MFIs are struggling to achieve financial sustainability. A long-term risk exists that these institutions may be unable to continue operations if this trend continues.

In addition to lack of repayment, MFIs report increased cases of funds going missing and loan officers deserting posts and stealing institutional funds. The temptation to engage in fraudulent behavior has increased given the ongoing liquidity crisis and the cash-based nature of microcredit lending. Managers of MFIs report an increased incidence of MFI staff not following established credit methodologies and pursuing connected lending (to friends or family).

The crisis has exposed the operational weaknesses of MFIs, which have contributed to poor lending practices for many institutions.

FIGURE I.3

Substantial Increase Observed in PAR over 30 Days among Iraqi and KRI MFIs, 2010–14

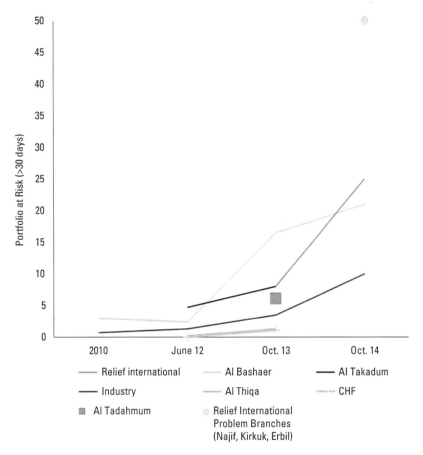

Source: Iraq Microfinance Network and MFIs, figures verified and cross-referenced although approximate.

Specifically, MFIs generally lack internal controls (legal and audit functions, AML/CFT procedures), have subpar credit assessment and reporting methodologies, provide inadequate training to build staff capacity, and lack governance systems to ensure accountability and transparency. These institutional practices are contributing to rising PARs and may threaten continued operations if not addressed.

The funding situation has worsened because of the ongoing instability. Although most MFIs have historically relied on grants, no new grants have been made to the sector since September 2012. Other sources of funding are limited. NGOs cannot raise equity or take deposits. Despite the absence of restrictions on fund transfers into and out of Iraq, international microfinance investors are not active in the country, with the exception of OPIC. Few local investors or banks appear to be willing to lend to MFIs. Some MFIs have reduced their outreach, stopped lending, and have stored working capital in reserve accounts because of the operational challenges related to the ongoing conflict.

A related and significant challenge is government oversight and regulation of the microfinance sector. The NGO law places NGOs under the NGO Directorate, which falls under Iraq's Council of Ministers. The NGO Directorate lacks the specialized knowledge of microfinance and understanding of credit, savings, and financial services necessary to provide appropriate oversight for the sector. The CBI, which has a better understanding and skills relating to financial services, does not currently play any role in overseeing MFIs. A stronger regulatory framework would better position public authorities to monitor MFIs in this current crisis context.

Potential of Microfinance Sector to Help Address the Economic and Social Impact of the Crisis in KRI

MFIs are reporting high demand for credit and financial services during this period of increased instability, particularly as clients seek tangible strategies to manage their financial needs, generate income, and smooth consumption in a general environment of declining economic activity and investor uncertainty. MFIs could play an important role in providing access to financial services during this period, particularly given the low levels of financial access and high levels of financial exclusion in Iraq and KRI. According to Global Findex data in 2011, only 10.6 percent of households of the adult population in Iraq had access to an account at a formal financial institution, the third lowest in the MENA region, and significantly below the regional average (17.7 percent) and income group average (57.2 percent). The high demand for microfinance services is also in part due to liquidity shortages of banks connected to the budget crisis between Baghdad and Erbil. Relief International, a leading KRI microfinance, recently provided $50,000 SME loans to two firms; this suggests that MFIs could also provide access to financial services to SMEs. However, given the financial constraints under which most NGO MFIs operate, it is unlikely that they will be able to meet increased client demand through their own resources.

IDPs represent a potential market segment for MFIs. Although MFIs interviewed reported being aware of the demand for microfinance among IDPs to generate short-term income, capacity, funding, and the high perceived risk profile of the segment have prevented MFIs from serving them to date. However, in light of the financial constraints of MFIs and the IDPs' risk profile, it is unlikely that MFIs would serve them without external support.

Recommendations

Short-Term Recommendations

We propose the following short-term recommendations:

- Provide assistance to well-managed MFIs in distress: Although the current crisis has had the strongest impact on MFIs with preexisting structural weaknesses, it has impacted well-functioning NGO MFIs through service disruptions in areas affected by violence, trade disruptions, and the KRG budget crisis, which has led to payment delays of government employees (clients and guarantors). The team recommends setting up a facility aimed at monitoring and providing assistance to well-managed MFIs that are in distress because of the ongoing crisis to ensure that they can continue providing essential financial services to their clients.[3] Assistance to MFIs in the area of internal controls, credit lending methodology, and operating in challenging conflict and fragile states would be important priorities.

- Bring MFIs under the supervision of a Financial Services Regulator: The current crisis has also accentuated weaknesses in the regulatory and supervisory framework, which could have helped to mitigate the impact of the crisis on MFIs. The NGO Directorate, which licenses NGO MFIs, lacks the capacity and knowledge to effectively monitor and supervise financial institutions. A well-trained financial sector supervisor could have helped identify and address some of the structural weaknesses (for example, governance and risk management) that have adversely affected a number of MFIs in recent months. Although the collapse of credit-only MFIs does not affect depositors and does not pose any systemic threat to the stability of the broader financial system, it would exclude a large number of low-income households from basic financial services, without any viable alternatives. The current regulatory framework is not well suited to monitor overindebtedness levels of clients and credit risk of clients, each of which has increased significantly in recent months.

- Place NGO MFIs under the supervision of the CBI: This seems to be the best placed regulator and supervisor of MFIs given its role as financial sector supervisor. In addition to the benefits of unified oversight of financial institutions, the CBI would be in a better position to advise NGO MFIs that seek to improve their governance and risk management, paving the way for a possible transformation into a finance company or even microfinance bank. If it is not possible for the CBI to regulate and supervise the NGO MFIs, then there needs to be strong coordination between the CBI and the NGO Directorate. The CBI may want to establish a dedicated unit focusing on the microcredit sector because their characteristics and oversight requires a very different approach from conventional commercial banks.

Medium- and Long-Term Recommendations

We make the following medium- and long-term recommendations:

- Allow for MFI transformation from associative status to finance companies: One of the key limitations that hinders NGO MFIs from expanding their financial services is their associative status: Although these NGOs were initially able to grow through donor support, they are now struggling to meet increasing client demand as donor resources have dwindled, preventing them from making the necessary investments in capital and infrastructure to meet growing client demand.

  Many countries address this funding challenge by allowing institutions to provide financial services as companies or banks, helping them raise capital, provide new services, and increase their outreach in a sustainable manner. This transformation also improves MFI governance and management through stricter regulatory requirements and oversight of shareholders. A similar path could be envisioned in Iraq but is currently obstructed by the reluctance of the NGO Directorate to allow for a transfer of assets from NGO MFIs to finance companies. The NGO law as written does not prohibit an NGO from selling its loan portfolio to a company in exchange for shares or money, provided that proceeds of the sale are used in accordance with the NGO's mission and that no personal gain is accrued from the sale by the NGO's members/founders and employees. The team recommends that the NGO Directorate considers the transformation of NGO MFIs to finance companies, in coordination with the CBI and the IMFN.

- Establish a comprehensive credit information sharing system: At present, banks and MFIs rely largely on personal guarantees of friends and family to assess the credit worthiness of borrowers and to secure their loans, a system that has several limitations. In addition to a longer and costlier process, relationship lending limits access to finance to wealthier populations and excludes groups who lack such ties or collateral. A well-run and accurate credit registry (public) or credit bureau (private) relies on the credit history of borrowers and can provide financial institutions with an inexpensive means of assessing the creditworthiness of many potential new borrowers, lowering transaction cost and time. This could potentially facilitate access to finance to domestic migrants and IDPs without personal ties in their new areas but with a solid credit history. In addition, credit bureaus can help financial institutions to better evaluate the financial health of existing clients, reducing risks of overindebtedness[4] and loan delinquency, which is particularly helpful in times of crisis. By applying a zero loan size reporting threshold permitting NGO MFIs to participate (which presumably would be possible if they were to be regulated by the CBI), the system will be useful for all financial institutions and not only banks. The participation of all financial institutions, including NGO MFIs, in the sharing system will also reduce the credit information gap.[5] In the interim, it would be useful to have a better developed information-sharing system among the MFIs managed by the Iraq Microfinance Network. In addition to an improved public credit registry, credit information could be further enhanced through the establishment of private credit bureaus. These often provide additional value-added services such as credit scores that help banks to better assess the creditworthiness of individuals and firms and ultimately enhance their access to financing.

- Conduct a demand study to assess current demand among low-income households for a variety of services, including credit, savings, payments and transfers, and insurance: Similar to other countries, a significant number of microfinance beneficiaries use the funds received from MFIs to cover personal financial needs such as emergencies, education, marriage, and consumption. However, very little information is at hand about the nature and magnitude of the demand for financial services, particularly for low-income households. A nationwide or KRI-specific comprehensive demand-side survey would be beneficial to better understand the demand for and usage of financial services by the poor, which could help the government to better address those needs.

- Expand the range of financial service providers and products for low-income households: Despite the absence of detailed demand-side information, available data from existing surveys (Findex) and interviews indicate that many needs of microfinance beneficiaries could be better met with financial products that are not available in the market: needs such as family emergencies (illness, death) through insurance, car and equipment purchase through leasing, education expenditures through student loans, and the like. Technical assistance could be mobilized quickly to help MFIs develop these products and better respond to the economic instability created by the ISIS conflict and refugee crisis.

Notes

1. State of Iraq's Microfinance Industry, USAID Tijara, October 2012, p. 3. USAID. 2012. "Provincial Economic Growth Program: State of Iraq's Microfinance Industry. "http://www.imfi.org/files/MFIs_Report_2012.pdf.
2. These "problem branches" are not a direct consequence of the ongoing crisis, but rather a consequence of the general fragility of the microfinance sector.
3. It will admittedly be very difficult to provide immediate assistance to MFIs in ISIS-controlled areas.
4. To avoid client overindebtedness through multiple loans, some jurisdictions require obtaining a client's credit report before granting a loan.
5. Article 51 of the Banking Law gives the CBI the authority to include any entity in the Credit Information System.

Poverty and Welfare Assessment: Methodology

A microsimulation model is developed for the purposes of this work to evaluate the welfare and distributional impacts of the Syrian refugee and IDP influx in the three governorates of KRI. This microsimulation method is a compromise between aggregate approaches and complex general equilibrium models. In the former, historical output and poverty trends are used to determine the responsiveness of poverty rates to growth in output (and consumption), which is then combined with macroeconomic projections to estimate the impacts of reduced growth on poverty. The latter, which are more sophisticated, such as Computable General Equilibrium models, involve general macroeconomic models that demand substantial information (for constructing social accounting matrices or time series of macroeconomic data) to create the "linkage aggregate variables" that are fed into the microsimulation model. Given the data available for KRI, and the observed inelasticity of poverty to growth, this compromise microsimulation approach is the most appropriate.

Given the particularities of the crisis in KRI, the major macroeconomic channels of impact are expected to work through (a) large changes in population, (b) changes in growth and employment, (c) changes in earnings, in particular, public sector salaries and public transfers, and (d) price changes. At the microlevel, the simulation uses information on (1) household-level income or consumption (or both), (2) household and individual characteristics, and (3) individual-level labor force and employment status and earnings, based on the Iraq Household and Socioeconomic Survey of 2012.

Several limitations and assumptions in applying this method are important to mention. First, the quality of projections from the model depends on the nature and accuracy of the data underpinning the exercise. The results would depend not only on the validity of the micromodels, but also on the macroprojections. In addition, the use of the last available household data (2012) as a comparator is tricky because the comparison could potentially attribute certain outcomes to that particular projection when they are a result of other factors that occurred over the period before 2012.

Second, the simulation relies on behavioral models built on past data that reflect the preexisting structure of the labor market, household incomes, and their relationships with demographics as they stood before the expected change. Consequently the simulation assumes these structural relationships remain constant over the period for which projections are made. The more distant in the past the baseline year is, the more questionable this assumption is likely to be.

This report presents estimates of impacts based on a "with-without" comparison, that is, the difference between with shock and without-shock scenarios for the years 2014 and 2015, using 2012—the year covered by the most recent household survey—as the baseline. Even though the microsimulation method allows modeling different types of shocks such as employment, earnings, or prices shocks, this exercise for the KRI will account only for different types of population shocks and assume that public transfers are not growing.

The lack of GDP and employment projections for KRI under different population shocks is the reason for focusing only on these types of impacts. The implication of making this decision is using the same projected GRP for each projected year. In other words, the KRI economy is assumed to behave exactly the same under the same natural population growth or when it is affected by the addition of Syrian refugees and or the effect of IDPs. However, the labor market is the only market that will be adjusted to account for population growth. Note that given the lack of information, output-employment elasticities would be assumed to remain constant across scenarios.

Annotated Methodology:
Health Sector

TABLE K.1
Actual Expenditure Variables

Variable Number	Variable Name	Methodology for Estimation	Assumption	Assumption Justification
A1	Adjusted actual expenditure (dinars)	$2007\text{–}14_{\text{(first 6 months)}}$: Actual expenditure/$(1 + \text{Yearly inflation})$ $2014_{\text{(last 6 months)}}$: $A1_{2013} \times (\text{Average \% increase of } A1_{2011\text{–}2013}) - A1_{2014\text{(first 6 months)}}$ 2015: $A1_{(2014\text{ first 6 months})} + A1_{(2014\text{ last 6 months})} \times (\text{Average \% increase of } A1_{2011\text{–}13})$	Actual total expenditures do not account for influx of IDPs/refugees	1. Actual total expenditures were not adjusted to accommodate IDP/refugee influx given (1) agreed budget allocation of 17% transfer from federal government being constant; (2) insufficient data and unpredictable number and timing of arrival of IDP/refugees migrating to allow for anticipation and planning 2. Yearly health CPI as reported by KRSO
A2	Actual per capita expenditure (dinars)	$2007\text{–}11$: A1/host community population 2012: 75% $A1_{2012}$/ host community population + 25% $A3_{2012}$ + $A4_{2012}$ $2013\text{–}15$: $A3_{2013\text{–}15}$ + $A4_{2013\text{–}15}$		For 2012, the actual per capita expenditure of the first 9 months is estimated as that of previous years. The estimate differs for the expenditure for the last 3 months of 2012 when the Syrian refugees arrived
A3	PHC actual per capita expenditure (dinars)	$2007\text{–}11$: A2 × 0.2 $2012\text{–}14$: A1 × 0.2/(host community population + (P1 + P4 × 50%) + (P2 + P5 + P6 × 100%))	1. Assuming a PHC-hospital expenditure distribution of 20–80% 2. Assuming out-of-camp refugees and IDPs have the same level of PHC utilization than the host community 3. Assuming in-camp refugees utilize public health services 50% less than the host community	1. NHI Report based on a national sample 2. Barriers to access of public health services (for example, distance, discretionary fees) may force the most vulnerable out-of-camp IDPs/refugees to forgo care despite a high burden of disease 3. In addition to barriers to access, UN humanitarian presence in the camps may have reduced in-camp refugees' and IDPs' seeking PHC outside the camps
A4	Hospital actual per capita expenditure (dinars)	$2007\text{–}11$: A2 × 0.8 $2012\text{–}15$: A1 × 0.8/(host community population + (P1 + P4 × 50%) + (P2 + P5 + P6 × 100%))	1. Assuming a PHC-hospital expenditure distribution of 20–80% 2. Assuming out-of-camp refugees and IDPs have the same level of hospital utilization than the host community 3. Assuming in-camp refugees utilize PHC services 50 percent less than the host community	1. NHI report based on a national sample 2. Barriers to access of PHC services (for example, distance, discretionary fees) may force the most vulnerable out-of-camp IDPs/refugees to forego care despite a high burden of disease 3. Based on referral rates of in-camp IDPs of a sample of six camps

TABLE K.2
Counterfactual Per Capita Expenditure Variables

Variable Number	Variable Name	Methodology for Estimation	Assumption	Assumption Justification
C1	PHC counterfactual per capita expenditure (dinars)	A1/host population × 0.20	1. The PHC-hospital budget allocation (20–80%) remained constant. 2. No Syrian refugee/IDP influx in KRI	No current or future policy reforms in place
C2	Hospital counterfactual per capita expenditure (dinars)	A1/host population × 0.80	1. The PHC-hospital budget allocation (20–80%) remained constant 2. No Syrian refugee/IDP influx in KRI	No current or future policy reforms in place

TABLE K.3
Population Variables

Variable Number	Variable Name	Methodology for Estimation	Assumption	Assumption Justification
P1	Syrian refugees in-camp	Total number of refugees × 0.44	90,000 Syrian refugees living inside 9 camps in 2014, implies that 44% of total Syrian refugees are living in camps. This distribution is assumed constant for 2012–15.	Jennings (2014)
P2	Syrian refugees out-of-camp	Total number of refugees × 0.56	90,000 Syrian refugees living inside 9 camps in 2014, implies that 44% of total Syrian refugees are living in camps. This distribution is assumed constant for 2012–15.	Jennings (2014)
P3	Total refugees		Not considering Syrian refugees in KRI-assisted areas	Jennings (2014)
P4	IDPs currently in-camp	Total number of IDPs × (number of IDP families in-camp / total number of IDP families)		Jennings (2014)
P5	IDPs to be relocated in camps	UN estimation of number of IDPs to be allocated in the 26 target camps	No additional camps (beyond the 26) will be built from October 2014 to December 2015	UN and KRG (2014a, b)
P6	IDPs out-of-camp	P7 – (P4 + P5)		UN and KRG (2014a, b)
P7	Total IDPs		Not considering IDPs in KRI-assisted areas	Jennings (2014)

TABLE K.4
Impact Assessment

Variable Number	Variable Name	Methodology for Estimation	Assumption	Assumption Justification
I1	PHC impact per capita (dinars)	2012: (A3 − C1)/4 2012−14: A3 − C1	Refugees migrated to KRI until October 2012 (last 3 months of 2012)	Jennings (2014)
I2	Hospital impact per capita (dinars)	2012: (A4 − C2)/4 2012−14: A4 − C2	Refugees migrated to KRI until October 2012 (last 3 months of 2012)	Jennings (2014)
I3	Total PHC impact (dinars)	I1 × host population		
I4	Total hospital impact (dinars)	I2 × host population		
I5	Total impact on host community (dinars)	I3 + I4		
I6	Grand total impact on host community (dinars)	$I5_{2012(last\ 3\ months)} + I5_{2013} + I5_{2014(first\ 6\ months)}$		
I7	Total impact on host community (dollars)	I5 / 1,160	Assuming exchange rate of $1 = ID 1,160	
I8	Grand total impact on host community (dollars)	I6 / 1,160	Assuming exchange rate of $1 = ID 1,160	

TABLE K.5
Stabilization Assessment

Variable Number	Variable Name	Methodology for Estimation	Assumption	Assumption Justification
SA1	Number of PHC extensions required	$(P2 + P6) / 5,000$		Based on Iraq standard of 1 PHC facility per 5,000 population
SA2	Capital cost to establish required PHC extensions for out-of-camp refugees (dinars)	$SA1 \times (8,000 \times 1,160) \times (P2/(P2+P6))$		Based on AMAR Foundation estimations of $8,000 per prefabricated extension of a PHC facility
SA3	Capital cost to establish required PHC extensions for out-of-camp IDPs (dinars)	$SA1 \times (8,000 \times 1,160) \times (P6/(P2+P6))$		
SA4	Subtotal capital cost to establish required PHC extensions for out-of-camp refugees and IDPs (dinars)	$SA2 + SA3$		
SA5	Stabilization recurrent cost for out-of-camp refugees (dinars)	$150\% (C1 + C2) \times P2$	Expecting that due to a higher burden of disease, PHC and hospital utilization levels of out-of-camp refugees will be 150% that of the host community	
SA6	Stabilization recurrent cost for out-of-camp IDPs (dinars)	$150\% (C1 + C2) \times P6$	Expecting that due to a higher burden of disease, PHC and hospital utilization levels of out-of-camp refugees will be 150% that of the host community	
SA7	Subtotal recurrent stabilization cost for out-of-camp refugees and IDPs (dinars)	$SA5 + SA6$		

(continued)

TABLE K.5 (*Continued*)

Variable Number	Variable Name	Methodology for Estimation	Assumption	Assumption Justification
SA8	Total stabilization cost for out-of-camp refugees and IDPs (dinars)	SA4 + SA7		
SA9	Total stabilization cost for out-of-camp refugees and IDPs (dollars)	SA8/1,160	Assuming exchange rate of $1 = ID 1,160	
SB1	PHC recurrent stabilization cost for in-camp refugees (dinars)	UN recurrent cost estimations × (P1 / (P1 + P4 + P5))	1. UN estimates for recurrent costs: assuming total running costs for PHC within camps of $8,546,673 for 12 months, which will cover: • Salaries of 46 mobile teams, with four staff each, and three shifts for MCH, TB, and surveillance/health promotion (assuming an average salary for staff of $500 a month) • Pharmaceuticals for mobile clinics • Salaries for 3 staff (including one doctor or assistant doctor and one nurse with an average salary for staff of $500 a month) per each of the 71 camps (using Iraq's standard of 1 PHC facility per 5,000 population) • Pharmaceuticals for PHC clinics 2. Assuming that P5 are relocated into camps	Based on UN and KRG (2014a, 2014b) cost estimates and needs assessment, and Iraq's standard of 1 PHC facility per 5,000 population
SB2	PHC recurrent stabilization cost for in-camp IDPs (dinars)	UN recurrent cost estimations × (P4 + P5 / (P1 + P4 + P5))	1. Assuming same UN estimations for recurrent costs as in SB1 2. Assuming that P5 are relocated into camps	Based on UN and KRG (2014a, 2014b) cost estimates and needs assessment, and Iraq's standard of 1 PHC facility per 5,000 population

(continued)

166

TABLE K.5 (*Continued*)

Variable Number	Variable Name	Methodology for Estimation	Assumption	Assumption Justification
SB3	Subtotal PHC recurrent stabilization cost for in-camp refugee and IDPs (dinars)	SB1 + SB2	Assuming that P5 are relocated into camps	
SB4	PHC capital cost for in-camp refugees (dinars)	2015: UN estimations for capital costs × (P1 / (P1 + P4 + P5))	1. Assuming an estimated $70,000 per mobile clinic (16 mobile clinics total, 1 per district) 2. Assuming an estimated $500,000 per prefabricated PHC clinic (71 PHC clinics total) 3. Assuming that P5 are relocated into camps.	UN and KRG (2014a, 2014b) and Iraq's standard of 1 PHC facility per 5,000 population
SB5	PHC capital cost for in-camp IDPs (dinars)	UN estimations for capital costs × ((P4 + P5) / (P1 + P4 + P5))	1. Assuming same UN estimations for capital costs as in SB4 2. Assuming that P5 are relocated into camps	UN and KRG (2014a, 2014b) and Iraq's standard of 1 PHC per 5,000 population
SB6	Subtotal PHC capital cost for in-camp refugees and IDPs (dinars)	SB6 + SB7		
SB7	Recurrent hospital cost for in-camp refugees (dinars)	150% C2 × P1	Expecting that due to a higher burden of disease, hospital utilization level of in-camp refugees will be 150% that of the host community	
SB8	Recurrent hospital cost for in-camp IDPs (dinars)	150% C2 × (P4 + P5)	Expecting that due to a higher burden of disease, hospital utilization level of in-camp refugees will be 150% that of the host community	
SB9	Subtotal recurrent hospital cost for in-camp refugees and IDPs (dinars)	SB7 + SB8		

(continued)

167

TABLE K.5 (*Continued*)

Variable Number	Variable Name	Methodology for Estimation	Assumption	Assumption Justification
SB10	Total stabilization cost for in-camp refugees and IDPs (dinars)	SB3 + SB6 + SB9		
SB11	Total stabilization cost for in-camp refugees and IDPs (dinars)	SB10/1,160	Assuming exchange rate of $1 = ID 1,160	
SC1	Medical equipment for refugees (dinars)	4,000,000 × 1,160 × (P3 / (P3 + P7))	Cost assumes medical supplies for hospital ICUs and smaller medical equipment for PHCs as estimated by the Department of Health ($4,000,000)	Interview with Department of Health
SC2	Medical equipment for IDPs (dinars)	4,000,000 × 1,160 × (P7 / (P3+ P7))	Cost assumes medical supplies for hospital ICUs and smaller medical equipment for PHCs as estimated by the Department of Health ($4,000,000)	Interview with Department of Health
SC3	Total medical equipment for refugees and IDPs (dinars)	SC1 + SC2		
SC4	Total medical equipment for refugees and IDPs (dollars)	SC3/1,160		
SD1	Cost of HMIS (dinars)		Assuming an estimated cost of $200 per staff trained in HMIS (assuming 600 trained staff)	Based on UN estimates
SD2	Cost of communication campaign materials (dinars)		Assuming an estimated cost of ID $116,000,000	Based on World Bank estimates of Turkmenistan communication campaign materials

(*continued*)

TABLE K.5 (*Continued*)

Variable Number	Variable Name	Methodology for Estimation	Assumption	Assumption Justification
SD3	Cost of rehabilitation (community mental health program) (dinars)		Assuming an estimated recurrent and training cost of $975,000 for the period of 15 months	Based on estimates provided by NGOs working on mental health in KRI, where the annual recurrent cost to cover all health care centers in KRI (two mental health professionals per center) is $600,000; and total training and mentoring cost of the staff is $180,000
SD4	Cost of immunization (dinars)		Assuming an estimated cost of $5,000,000 per one immunization campaign	Based on UN estimates of immunization campaigns in KRI
SD5	Programmatic stabilization cost for refugees (dinars)	$(SD1 + SD2 + SD3 + SD4) \times (P3 / (P3 + P7))$		
SD6	Programmatic stabilization cost for IDPs (dinars)	$(SD1 + SD2 + SD3 + SD4) \times (P7 / (P3 + P7))$		
SD7	Total programmatic stabilization cost for refugees and IDPs (dinars)	$SD5 + SD6$		
SD8	Total programmatic cost for refugees and IDPs (dollars)	$SD7 / 1,160$	Assuming exchange rate of $1 = ID 1,160	

Note: HMIS = Health Management and Information System; ICU = intensive care unit; IDP = internally displaced person; KRSO = Kurdistan Regional Statistics Office; MCH = maternal and child health; NGO = nongovernmental organization; PHC = primary health care; TB = tuberculosis; UN = United Nations.

Bibliography

Brookings Institute. 2007. "Iraq Index Tracking Variables of Reconstruction and Security Post-Saddam Iraq."

Central Organization for Statistics and Information Technology (COSIT), the Kurdistan Region Statistics Office (KRSO) and the Nutrition Research Institute of the Ministry of Health (NRI) with Technical Support from UNICEF, WFP and FAO. 2010. "Food Insecurity in Iraq."

Cohen, R. 2000. "Reintegrating Refugees and Internally Displaced Women." Conference on Intra-State Conflicts and Women, December.

Cordoba, Armando. 2013. "Kurdistan Erbil Attack: The One That Got Through."

De Berry, Joanna P., and Benjamin Petrini. 2011. "Forced Displacement in Europe and Central Asia," October. World Bank, Washington, DC.

Dombey, Daniel, Shawn Donnan, and John Reed. 2014. "Isis Advance Reverses Decade of Growth in Middle East Trade." Ft.com, July 2.

Economist Intelligence Unit. 2014. "Benchmarking the Kurdistan Region."

FAO and the World Bank. 2012. "Iraq Agricultural Sector Note."

Global Trade Information Services. 2014. Global Trade Atlas.

International Monetary Fund. 2013. "Iraq-Article IV Consultation." IMF Country Report No. 13/217, Washington, DC.

International Organization for Migration. 2014. "Response to the IDP Crisis in Iraq: Displacement Tracking Matrix."

Invest In Group – KRG Department of Foreign Relations. 2014. "Kurdistan Review 2013."

Iraq Body Count. 2014. Iraq Body Count Database. https://www.iraqbodycount.org

Iraq Central Statistical Organization and World Bank. 2007. "Iraq Household Socio-Economic Survey (IHSES)."

Iraq Ministry of Planning and Central Statistical Organization. 2013. "Environment in Numbers."

Jennings, R. 2014. "Baseline Contextual Analysis of Forced Displacement in the Kurdistan Region of Iraq: Scope, Movements, Contextual Factors." World Bank, Washington, DC.

KRG. 2001. "Socio-Economic Infrastructure Factsheet."

KRG. 2006. "Law of Investment in KRG – Iraq." Law No. (4).

KRG. 2012a. "Electricity Sector Economic and Financial Analysis Report." June.

KRG. 2012b. "Economic and Financial Analysis Report."

KRG. 2012c. "Kurdistan Highway Master Plan."

KRG. 2013. "Kurdistan Road Asset Management."

KRG. 2014. "Kurdistan Region: 2013 Facts and Figures."

KRG Ministry of Natural Resources. 2014. Press Release, May 26.

KRG Ministry of Planning and UNDP. 2012. "Building the Kurdistan Region of Iraq – The Socio-Economic Infrastructure."

KRG – United Nations. 2014. "Kurdistan Region of Iraq (KR-I) Has Become a Refuge from Iraq's Violence."

KRG Ministry of Planning. 2013. "Kurdistan Region of Iraq 2020: A Vision for the Future."

KRG Ministry of Labor and Social Affairs. 2013. "KRG Progress Report, 2009-2013."

KRSO and UNICEF. 2011. "The Evolution of the Situation of Children and Women in the Kurdistan Region of Iraq."

Kurdistan Regional Statistics Office (KRSO). 2012. "Labor Force Survey Report." Iraq.

Kurdistan Regional Statistics Office (KRSO). 2013. "Labor Force Survey Report." Iraq.

RAND. 2014. "Strategic Priorities for Improving Access to Quality Education in the Kurdistan Region, Iraq."

REACH. 2014. "Iraq IDP Crisis Overview."

Ross Anthony, C., Melinda, Moore, Lee H. Hilborne, and Andrew W. Mulcahy. 2014. "Health Sector Reform in the Kurdistan Region, Iraq. Financing Reform, Primary Care, and Patient Safety." RAND Corporation.

SEINA-UNDP. 2012a. "Socio-Economic Infrastructure Needs Assessment for Kurdistan Region—Water Supply and Sanitation Infrastructure."

SEINA-UNDP. 2012b. "Socio-Economic Infrastructure Needs Assessment (SEINA) in KRG, Agricultural Sector, Moving from a Subsidized Agriculture to a Competitive Agriculture."

UNDP and KRG Ministry of Planning. 2012. "Building the Kurdistan Region of Iraq."

UN–HABITAT. 2012. "Socio-Economic Infrastructure Needs Assessment Project in Kurdistan." Transport Infrastructure Report.

UNHCR. 2013. "Countries Hosting Syrian Refugees: Solidarity and Burden Sharing - Background Paper for the High Level Segment – Provisional Release."

UNHCR. 2014a. "Global Appeal 2014-2015 Middle East and North Africa, Regional Summary."

UNHCR. 2014b. "Syria Regional Response Plan."

UNHCR/REACH. 2014a. "Multi-Sector Needs Assessment of Syria Refugees Living Outside Camps in the Kurdistan Region of Iraq."

UNHCR/REACH. 2014b. "Shelter and CCM Cluster Rapid Assessment: Iraq Internal Displacement Crisis Assessment."

UNHCR and IOM. 2013. "Iraq: The Impact of the Syrian Crisis."

UNICEF. 2013. "One in Ten in School: An Overview of Access to Education for Syrian Refugee Children and Youth in the Urban Areas of the Kurdistan Region of Iraq (KRI)." Report Prepared by NRC Iraq. Norwegian Refugee Council.

United Nations and KRG Ministry of Planning. 2014a. "Immediate Response Plan for the IDPs Crisis in the KRI for the Period of 15 September – 15 November 2014."

United Nations and KRG Ministry of Planning. 2014b. "Immediate Response Plan Phase II (IRP2) for Internally Displaced People in the Kurdistan Region of Iraq for the Period of 15 November 2014- 31 March 2015." December.

United Nations, NGOs, and KRG. 2012. "Rapid Needs Assessment of Syrians in the Kurdistan Region of Iraq."

United Nations Office for the Coordination of Humanitarian Affairs. 2014a. "Iraq Crisis: Situation Report." No.12.

United Nations Office for the Coordination of Humanitarian Affairs. 2014b. "Iraq Humanitarian Profile."

United Nations World Food Program. 2013. "Syrian Refugees and Food Insecurity in Iraq, Jordan, and Turkey: Secondary Literature and Data Desk Review."

United Nations World Food Program. 2014. "Vulnerability Analysis and Mapping of Food Security and Nutrition Database (VAM)."

United Nations World Food Program and Government of Iraq. 2012. "Food Security, Living Conditions and Social Transfers in Iraq."

WFP-CSO-KRSO. 2012. "Food Security, Living Conditions and Social Transfers in Iraq."

World Bank. 2011a. "Azerbaijan: Building Assets and Promoting Self Reliance: The Livelihoods of Internally Displaced Persons." World Bank, Washington, DC.

World Bank. 2011b. *World Development Report: Conflict, Security, and Development.* Washington, DC: World Bank.

World Bank. 2012. "Public Expenditure Review: Towards More Efficient Spending for Better Service Delivery in Iraq." World Bank, Washington, DC.

World Bank. 2014. "Poverty, Inclusion and Welfare in Iraq, 2007–2012." World Bank, Washington, DC.

World Bank and UNHCR. 2011. "Research Study on IDPs in Urban Settings – Afghanistan."

World Bank Enterprise Survey, Iraq. 2011.

World Health Organization. 2008. "Iraq National Health Accounts." WHO, Geneva, Switzerland.